QUIT YOUR JOB BEFORE IT KILLS YOU

28 TIPS TO EMPOWER YOURSELF, GET UNCOMFORTABLE, FIGHT FEAR AND FIRE YOUR NARCISSISTIC BOSS

JOSEPH COHEN

WWW.QUITANDWIN.COM

© Copyright *Joseph Cohen* 2021 – All rights reserved.

The content contained within this book may not be reproduced, duplicated, or transmitted without direct written permission from the author or the publisher.

Under no circumstances will any blame or legal responsibility be held against the publisher, or author, for any damages, reparation, or monetary loss due to the information contained within this book. Either directly or indirectly. You are responsible for your own choices, actions, and results.

Legal Notice:

This book is copyright protected. This book is only for personal use. You cannot amend, distribute, sell, use, quote or paraphrase any part, or the content within this book, without the consent of the author or publisher.

Disclaimer Notice:

Please note the information contained within this document is for educational and entertainment purposes only. All effort has been executed to present accurate, up to date, and reliable, complete information. No warranties of any kind are declared or implied. Readers acknowledge that the author is not engaging in the rendering of legal, financial, medical, or professional advice. The content within this book has been derived from various sources. Please consult a licensed professional before attempting any techniques outlined in this book.

By reading this document, the reader agrees that under no circumstances is the author responsible for any losses, direct or indirect, which are incurred because of the use of the information contained within this document, including but not limited to, errors, omissions, or inaccuracies.

CONTENTS

Introduction — 11

0. The Jump — 15
1. The Salt Mine and The Narcissist — 19
2. The Man – Never Enough — 28
3. Ready to Face the Challenge…and Walk Away — 44
4. Don't Quit, Ever — 50
5. Challenge vs. Opportunity — 58
6. The Super Ugly Example — 61
7. Next Stop - Discomfort — 75
8. The Free Fall — 78
9. Shared Identity — 83
10. Growth in the Face of "No" — 94
11. 15 Minute Manifesto — 99
12. Warm Interlude — 103
13. Inspiration vs. Intimidation — 107
14. Sugar — 117
15. The Plan — 120
16. Time to Quit? — 128
17. Comfortably Numb (Fooling Yourself) — 133
18. Dysfunction — 146
19. Sweet Sugar — 152
20. The Move and the Plan — 160
21. Time to Stop — 167
22. The Pearl that Drops out of the Poop — 184
23. Ride Share — 195
24. Inspirational Rides — 200
25. Taking the Leap — 217

26. Free at Last	221
27. The Landing	227
Conclusion	231
Acknowledgments	239
About the Author	243

A Special Gift To Our Readers

The SWOT Checklist

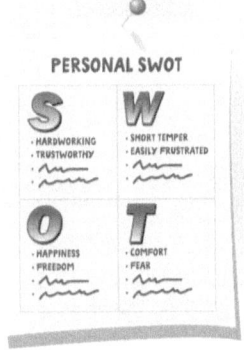

Included with your purchase of this book is our personal SWOT Challenge. This challenge will strategically help you discover what you want the next step in your life to be.

Click the link below and let us know which email address to deliver it to.

www.quitandwin.com

To my family and friends, your love and support inspires me every day. Thank you!

To all the employees, you don't have to persevere through an uninspiring job and a bad boss. All you have to do is believe in yourself, quit, and go after what YOU want!

"Most people work just hard enough not to get fired and get paid just enough money not to quit."

— GEORGE CARLIN

INTRODUCTION

It's time to quit! It's time to move on! We know it in our guts and we've put up with enough. It's time to stop persevering, enduring, and pushing through whatever challenges we are faced with and walk away from the jobs we hate. It is not worth it!

We have nothing else left to prove and we only have our happiness at stake. We've been putting up with a job we loathe, a boss we can no longer work for, and a profession that is uninspiring. We are miserable. So, what's stopping us? We have justifiable reasons for why we should run out of that building and away from that job, that career. But we still show up every morning to do something we hate for someone we hate even more. Do we think that if we left, we would be labelled a "quitter" or, worse yet, a failure? Are we losers for walking away? Is the prospect of financial hardship a deterrent to freeing ourselves? Does it scare the daylights out of us to be without a paycheck? All those questions are completely legitimate considerations. We have family who depend on us. We have bills to pay. So, we trade our happiness to keep on going. Is that a fair trade? We tell ourselves that happiness wasn't that important anyway. How satisfied does that realization make us feel? It doesn't at all, does it?

Let's take the "if" challenge about our job situation. See how many times you answer "yes" to the statements below. The more you answer "yes," the more you are going to have to get comfortable with an uncomfortable decision.

> "If" it is Monday and you can't wait for Friday, it's time to quit.
> "If" you have a boss who doesn't recognize your efforts with a simple "thanks," it's time to quit.
> "If" you never feel like you've done enough, it's time to quit.
> "If" work feels more like a chore, it's time to quit.
> "If" you constantly watch the clock's hands creep through the day, it's time to quit.
> "If" one day at work feels like an entire month…well, you know the answer.

How many times did you say yes to the above scenarios? It is a simple test with a simple decision, but you still won't make the decision you know in your gut you have to make.

We are not quitting because we are comfortable; we are miserably comfortable. Being able to pay those bills is a legitimate trade-off. Of course, it is. Work is not supposed to be fun anyway, right? It's a job. Nothing more and nothing less. Suck it up and carry on doing what you are supposed to be doing! We know what we have with our crappy job, but we don't know what we have without it. We are not quitting because we are scared. What happens when we leave what we know for the unknown? Unfamiliarity is scary. The grass is not always greener on the other side of the fence. You could quit and be more miserable and uninspired than you are now. That would be one hell of a trade! Add in the stress from all the responsibilities, obligations, and expectations we have, as well as the societal pressure to rise to meet every challenge or risk being a loser who quits, and, well…we ain't going nowhere!

But there is hope. First, you aren't the only one who feels this way. You are not the first person to go through this. You are not the only "worker" who goes to work uninspired. Fortunately, a lot of people have gone through this garbage experience, and while misery does love company, the people who have made the decision to walk away have come out better and can share that it is not as bad as your fearful imagination is making it. This book provides such affirmation. It shares a journey that so many of us have gone through. It distills the experience into relatable chunks so that you can recognize what you are going through and then take action by choosing a similar, healthy path. Along with the story are 28 "pearls" that our character picked up on his journey which may be applicable to your own situation. Use these "pearls" to plan your escape toward your personal path to happiness.

Quitting is important. You don't have to go through hell. You only have one life. Don't waste a precious moment in a thankless job working for an ungrateful boss.

This book is about making the courageous decision to quit, which may be initially uncomfortable but will ultimately offer lifelong rewards and happiness. What is more important than that?! It is the answer, and it is right in front of you. Take it. It is all about letting go, trusting your instinct in your misery, and going for it. Let go of the ego, insecurities, and the comfort. You have no idea how incredibly talented and worthy you are until you jump out of your miserable situation.

For most of my career, I held on tight to my job and it cost me dearly despite all the success I had achieved. My mistake of not quitting sooner, when my gut was screaming at me to do so, and the lessons gained from finally choosing happiness is what this book is all about. This story is about an executive who has an epiphany that what he was most afraid of was the answer to all his problems.

So, take a deep breath and get ready to jump. You've got this!

0. THE JUMP

Gary's toes peaked just over the edge of the doorway. They curled in his shoes with a grip that was strengthened by excitement, anxiety, and fear. Right below those tightly curled toes was twelve-thousand feet of air – a pale blue sky painted by yellow sunshine and the blooming earth below. The air stirred into a forceful wind, and it swept right through him taking his breath away. He swallowed hard. Was he really going to do it? Every inch of his body felt electric. Every hair on his skin was standing at attention and every muscle gripped onto every bone in his body. The sound around him was deafening. The plane propellers cut through the air relentlessly like a machine gun that obliterated all other sound. He looked back at the empty seat he had just left before he readied his helmet and his parachute rig. That seat was now lonely, and he wanted, in the worst way, to go keep it company.

Calmness and safety were lounging around there. He could easily step back into the comfort of the plane and be completely disappointed in himself, but at least he would be back to being comfortable. It was familiar! It was better to know what he knew, live there, and make love to it. The devil known versus the devil unknown, right? The answer seemed to be a resounding "hell yes" at that very instant. Everyone knew that. It was safe inside the plane.

There was nothing to lose in the comfort, nothing to fear. But he knew there was another "nothing" at play in the world of comfort. There was nothing to be gained. He knew it. Damn it! He was getting stale in that comfort seat. Moldy toast! While it fit him like a nice pair of silk underwear, it wasn't doing him any favors. Comfort made for the perfect black and white movie. Life in color wasn't even a whisper of comfort. Why would you dare step outside of comfort's lovely, mesmerizing, and sultry bosom?

He knew nothing about jumping out of a plane. He stood at the doorway of the twin-engine King Air ready to mark one more item off his bucket list and push himself to the limits of fear. Hell, there was no turning back now. That choice left long ago. There was something prompting his soul to jump out of the plane and into the fear that gave strength to the iron clench his toe grip had at the door's edge. Time to strip off that silk underwear. What he didn't know was that the step out of the plane would not be the leap he thought it would. The greatest step had already been taken long before he even got on the plane. That step was the commitment to jump out of a plane in the first place. The courage to challenge his comfort limits was born at that point. Every other step afterward, even though he didn't feel it at the edge of the doorway, was more like gliding. That leap out of the plane was more like a lean, anyway. Just a small lean forward and a simple matter of letting go. Letting go of the silk underwear. Letting go of fear and believing in himself. All that was left was belief – no effort required. He took a deep breath, centered himself in his quaking body, closed his eyes and leaned forward.

The Pearl: Shed the trance of comfort and get ready for the pearls that come from being uncomfortable. It is never as bad as fear imagines. Have trust in your jump. You've got this!

1

THE SALT MINE AND THE NARCISSIST

Gary was once again standing and staring but this time the view wasn't an incredible vision out of a plane's doorway. It was himself, dressed in a suit and tie in the office bathroom. "Why am I staying here? What is wrong with me? Why won't I jump? This place is killing me," he said to his reflection in the bathroom mirror. It was 7 pm on a Friday. Just outside of the bathroom was an empty office. All the lights were off, and all the desks vacated. All that awaited his exit from his confessional was deafening silence.

Gary's office was a place that had never seen better days. It was dated, ragged, and abused. Four walls inhabited by third-hand cubicles. The innovative and chic décor of 21st Century workspaces that incorporate Barcaloungers, ergonomic desks, office cafes, big LCD monitors and liberal dress codes, was not an environment Gary and his coworkers ever knew. On top of that, the boss always reminded them how lucky they were to work in such a place. Since most of them started their careers there, they were thankful and never realized that what they were working in was not standard office luxury.

Office space is 100 percent representative of the owner. The place was nothing less than a mirror image of his boss's essence. The office was a homage the boss had built to himself. It was masculine. It was simple and austere. It had motivational posters of coercive encouragement on every wall about how to never compromise, never apologize, reach new limits, and fight hard as well as other assorted propaganda the boss thought would inspire his employees.

This organization with authoritarian rule drained the souls of its employees for someone else's profit. Desk, phone, and a water fountain – what else did a person selling high-tech products really need? Anything more and they would be entitled, spoiled brats! Our main character was born and raised here. He never knew differently. Hostility, scrutiny, thanklessness, and no creature comforts were his normal. He made his home here, clueless to the reality that in the 21st century, these places were becoming extinct. He called this place the Salt Mine and the people that worked there were simple miners.

His boss also had several wooden plaques put up strategically around the walls of the salt mine, each with just a single word. Ironically, that one word made everyone not think. The miners unanimously agreed that it was just a slap in the face, confirming that the boss thought they were incompetent and stupid. Employees would walk by these plaques, glance at them and then just flat out get pissed. Five letters, one word - "Think." Yes, it was everywhere. The boss thought it would inspire his people. Nevertheless, everyone knew that when a "Think" plaque went up a mistake had been made. Instead of embracing the circumstances and inspiring improvement, the boss would put another plaque up on the wall. There it was in the breakroom, above the printer and even in the bathroom, that five-letter word, etched in classic Times New Roman font, staring down at everyone. Gary always felt that he had no need to do any thinking at the urinal. He thought he had that covered.

The constant reminders to think only created animosity. Employees didn't want to give the boss any sense that his demeaning management technique was working. They couldn't really explain it, but those plaques made them act out like indignant, rebellious school kids who were told they were bad. Everybody in the company played the part. Therefore, more and more "think" signs went up and less and less progress was made as an act of defiance. Constant misjudgment crushes morale. Why try to prove the boss's negative impression wrong? The punishment for doing better was the reinforcement of the boss's wall art campaign.

As long as a miner was making the boss money, they were golden. If they weren't performing up to the boss's standard, they got the cold shoulder. They always knew someone's job was in trouble when the boss wouldn't even acknowledge that person's existence. He would walk right by them and not even look at them. They were dead to him. Worse still, they were alive, a living and breathing human being, treated as if they shouldn't even have bothered getting out of bed. They were a ghost taking up space and air. What a disappointment! What a management technique by "the Man."

Gary's boss was definitely the Man. By his own admission, he had excelled and achieved more than anyone could have ever dreamed. He was the Man because that's what he thought of himself. He was a better, smarter, faster, and slyer know-it-all with soft hands and an aggressive disposition. Question the Man and they all were in trouble. Compliment the Man and they privately owned him. The employees, or rather miners, also knew him as the Man. They had their own definition: the enforcer, big brother, and the narcissist. He was the person capable of making them pay if they made a mistake and the person who thought they didn't "think." They could never measure up to him in their wildest dreams.

If they wanted to have a conversation with the Man, they had to perform. If they wanted any comradery with him, they had better sell; otherwise, they were just using up oxygen and occupying a spot on a seat. If they wanted direction or leadership, they had better prepare themselves to hear the Man's heroic salesmanship stories from 40 years ago. He never made them feel like they did enough and as a result, they were eventually gone. Their days were numbered the day they started work. He wouldn't fire them though. He couldn't have the unemployment obligation on his hands. He would just make it so "icy" and miserable that they had to leave. Voila, the salt mine!

Another week was done. Another 7 pm. Another Friday evening bathroom stare down. Gary didn't even look at the "think" sign in the bathroom. The bright white fluorescent lights shone above him, reflecting off the bright white walls surrounding him. It was blinding yet dull. His image in the mirror was challenging him. He stood there in the company bathroom alone, staring at himself. He was tired, so tired – the type of tired that made him want to cry but he couldn't coax a tear. It wasn't that he was physically exhausted; it was emotional exhaustion that ground him to a paralyzing and numbing trance. He got a sneak peak of what was happening to his soul. The image in front of him was frightening. His own stare went right through him, grabbed his heart, and squeezed. He sighed. The breath rushed out of his lips and took thoughts of "why" with it into the air. This was not about taking a leap of faith out of an airplane. This was a lot scarier than that. This was so personal. He no longer recognized who he was looking at even though he had spent his entire life examining his own reflection. Gary's imposing six-foot-five, 275-pound frame somehow reflected a child half that height and half that weight. At least the emotionally exhausted image in the mirror stared back at him with empathy and compassion. What a day! Another Friday evening that bore into him and spit out excrement, leaving him hollow. He wore hollow like an old, comfortable shoe. He always had that empty feeling of having had enough. He couldn't feel or even try. Why bother? It wouldn't matter anyway. He tried composing himself even though the fight in him was gone. He didn't know what to do but just stand, stare, and breathe.

His 20 years at the salt mine took a toll on him. His desk job made him feel and look like a mineworker who had just come up from a long, lengthy day of backbreaking labor smashing rocks in a cauldron of hell fire. His sales job was killing him, or to put it more precisely, the owner, his boss, "the Man" whose heyday had been nearly half a century ago, was killing him.

His weariness was topped with a nice healthy dash of sad. A better word than "sad" should probably be used here. Any of the big "D" words in its place seemed more appropriate: demoralized, devastated, desperate, disappointed. But "sad" was simple and easier to say and understand. It landed on him deeply and resonated. He related to it intimately. "Sad" combined all those gloomy "D" words in a beautifully wrapped present with a dreary grey bow on top.

What happened? Why was he continuing to play this game with this bully? Was he simply enduring? Life should never be endured. He knew that! He didn't have time for that, no one did! He had one life. As he stared back at himself, it was evident, that it was time to stop. It was time to stop simply surviving and start living. Time to lean out and jump...again!

"I've got to quit this," he said quietly to himself. Maybe Gary's real problem was that he was "thinking" too much. Maybe it was time to have faith in his gut. His exasperation was a perfect foundation for the anger that was building in him. He was mad at himself. He clenched his jaw and stared more intently at the mirror image. What was he still doing here? "I've got to quit," he repeated more sternly to himself.

His company and the Man made him feel marginalized. He felt unappreciated and undermined. He knew that he was responsible for his own feelings and that no one or nothing should be given the power over another's own disposition or shit storm. But fuck! It was hard not to be completely infected by the toxicity of the salt mine. He was finally inviting himself to his very own pity party. How pathetic! Amazing what one place, one job and one man could do to degrade another man to a point that he felt this way. He let it happen. True, he was not faced with a matter of life or death, but wasn't that what mattered? He was faced with a matter of his own existence and self-worth – his own happiness. There was no denying that the place and the Man were slowly tearing up his soul. How many other people in the workplace felt the same way? Probably millions. People just breathing deep, enduring, sucking it up, making a buck, day in and day out, leaving happiness on the pillow as they got up to go to their very own salt mine. Why? Made no damn sense. He had been a pure professional at doing just that for his entire career!

"When was it ever going to be enough?" he thought as he loosened his tie. What was it going to take for him to make a change? He was disappointing himself daily by not doing enough to recognize that he had to leave the poisonous mine. On top of his own disappointment was the Man's incessant daily drumbeat that he was never doing "enough"! "Enough" was burying him. If striving to meet the Man's definition of "enough" didn't kill him, his own inability to say "enough" would. He was a slave to the Man and a slave to his own blind dedication and persistence. Enough!

The Pearl: If you are constantly compromising, you are enduring life. That is the first sign and the only sign you need to be aware of to make a change. Listen to your heart, shut off your mind, and trust your gut. Quit to win!

2

THE MAN – NEVER ENOUGH

The weekly mirror stare-down occurred every Friday evening. This was no "get psyched", "get pumped", "ra ra ra" stare down. The day was over. The ambush just finished. Not a lot to get pumped up for. No one else was around in the office…again. It was just him and the guy in the mirror. While the salt mine employed incredible people, who worked as long as needed on other days, Friday, 5:01pm was different. It was quitting time. The long hours of the week gave way to the freedom of the weekend. Everyone had jettisoned themselves out of the place as quickly as possible to get on with their respective lives. Weekends had no resemblance to the previous five days. They dove into their weekends just as they had dived into their weekdays – with determination. It was a sales organization filled with ambitious, hustling, alpha types, and initiative-driven conquerors. These people worked hard and played even harder. They put such lofty expectations on themselves that by the end of the week, they were big fat balloons ready to pop. "Let them pop – they deserved it," Gary always thought. He loved his people. He admired them, he trusted them, he believed in them. Who cares if when 5:01pm on a Friday came around, they left him alone?

He wanted them to have a reprieve because he knew that Monday was lurking and the quicker they could all decompress from the intensity of the place, the faster they could face Monday and have the energy and compulsion to do it all over again. Getting out of the place also let them "think" whenever and wherever they wanted.

The Man, who considered himself one of the best salespersons on the planet for the past 40 years, could never understand the empty office. Leaving at 5:01pm, even on a Friday, was sacrilegious. The Man got a masochistic rush every day at quitting time. He liked to troll the sales floor right before 5 o'clock to keep those salespeople from jetting out at 5pm. He got off on that. He also loved to judge them as he watched them walk out to their cars early. What he never acknowledged was that they were already riddled with guilt for leaving at 5pm. They didn't need his judgement. That was just the type of people they were. Whether it was self-induced or boss-inflicted, they usually left work feeling like they hadn't done enough.

But Gary was still at the office, in the bathroom, staring at himself as the complete silence competed with the running urinal he had just left behind. He just finished enduring another Friday evening debrief with the Man. It happened every Friday – the weekly debrief which more closely resembled a perfectly orchestrated cavity search conducted by the maestro. These interrogations seemed reasonable and innocent enough at the beginning of Gary's career. Gary even understood the value of the cavity searches, mostly. But as they continued to occur every Friday evening, he began to understand these end-of-the-week traps as just an opportunity for the Man to expound on how he could have done better and how it was always done better back in the day when he controlled the herd.

Funny how Gary never saw that as part of the initial job description. Interogatee! Is that even a word? Hell, there were a lot of things the Man hadn't told him when he was first being recruited. First and foremost, the job description should have mentioned:

"You must interact daily and have a post-week, late night debrief with a clinical narcissist."

Gary wondered if he would have taken the job if he knew that was going to be the primary requirement. His position title should have been "Chief Narcissist Whisperer" instead of Director of Sales. Initially, this weekly event was as innocent as a simple drop of water falling to the ground. But, as each meeting occurred and another drop fell, the puddle became a pond, then a lake, and eventually an ocean of pressure that put Gary on the verge of drowning. The Man smiled.

Friday evenings worked out perfectly for the Man. The Man never looked forward to the weekend. The weekend wasn't a formal workday, and if it wasn't a workday, it was meaningless. The Man had the country club and the status to uphold. The Man always boasted about how much time he put in on

Saturdays and Sundays and then waited to be praised. If they didn't respond in kind with the same sort of effort, he would judge them.

The weekly debriefs, or rather the cavity searches – the 12-round sparring sessions – always started with, "Did you...?" The answers that Gary gave always began and ended in, "Yes." They had to. Gary didn't say "yes" simply to avoid the return punch that came with a "no" answer. He perfected his skills to be sure that he had all the bases covered. He did not want to get blindsided or tripped up and give the Man any reason to demean him or stand over him like a prize fighter over a knockout. So, the Man's scrutiny, a purely negative experience, was the tool Gary used to sharpen and hone his skills. He embraced and benefited from this regular sparring with the Man. The scrutiny made him work hard on the details. He had to cover every angle and explore every option. It was all about anticipating every punch from his adversary. He bristled with pride when he was able to duck in time and counter with his own swing. It was the only way to survive the talks and establish any credibility. Gary was okay with that exercise. But for the Man the real motivation for the exercise was to reinforce his perceived superiority and to prevent his own relevance from flat lining. Had the Man known that this exercise would be improving Gary's business acumen by sharpening his awareness and instincts, he would have chosen a different tactic for sure. Over time, the Man's suspicion grew, and he began realizing that he was creating a monster –

someone who threatened his relevance in his own company. While he was benefitting from Gary's improved ability, he saw his own impact on the business diminishing. In Gary's mind, this unintentional ritual was becoming a gift that he was to use against the Man as they continued to build the business together.

While questions came at him like the rapid fire of a machine gun, the exercise made him look at things from a different perspective and made his own skills sharper. How? Gary had to have all angles covered – even the ones that were completely irrational and never going to happen. Having to be so intently focused gave Gary a habit of looking at everything with a 360-degree vision. Gary was thankful for the lesson because it made him tirelessly methodical and detailed in running his operation. The consequence of the incessant examination of a "no" answer was that he either honed his skills, actions, goals, and abilities or became roadkill. He had to have all the bases covered or he was in for a long Friday night interrogation. "Bring it on! I am better for it," Gary always felt.

However, Gary utterly loathed what followed – the story. He would have to sit through an epic tale of how the Man would have done it differently followed by wonderful descriptive examples of how he regularly saved the day. The Man had a sturdy back from all the shoulder patting he gave himself. The Man never avoided an opportunity to self-indulge and verbally flagellate. Every time the Man went into one of his stories, Gary felt like an elephant walked up to him, smiled, and then sat down on his chest.

Gary's "yeses" weren't lies just to avoid giving the Man self-tooting opportunities. While the sessions were tough, having to sit and listen to someone talk about how wonderful he was all the time was the mind-numbing calisthenics Gary wanted to avoid. So, Gary was tireless in predicting every question that would be asked so that he could address every perceived need and respond with resounding "yeses" to the questions he knew of and the ones he thought could crawl out of the Man's skull. Gary was better for it. This skill that was honed from this torturous Friday debrief was the pearl that he had discovered. Gary never got any praise for all the "Yeses." He just got more questions that challenged his efforts and accomplishments. The Man would not be outdone. He wanted to catch a "no" there somewhere. He had to. He privately got off on it. No one could dare think they were as good as he was or had thought through everything like he would. He loved to hear himself give advice. He was the top dog and that would always be reiterated as long as any answers were anything but a "yes."

The Man's scrutiny dripped down on to miner's work too:

The Man: Did you talk with Erica about upping her number of daily calls?

Gary: Yes.

The Man: Did you see the dress she had on?

"Really?", Gary thought.

Gary: Yes

The Man: Did you interview Tom and give him an offer?

Gary: Yes

The Man: Did you handle the sponsorship from company "ABC" that dealt with event "DEF"?

Gary: Yes

The Man: Did you sell customer "GHI" on our benefits versus competitor "JKL"?

Gary: Yes

The Man: What's up with James?

Gary: Well, James closed a beautiful deal for $600k. He really did a great job landing and closing it.

The Man: What else did James do?

"Well, I publicly thanked James. I gathered the department together and we had a toast to mark and celebrate the hard-earned sale. I gave him the rest of the day off. He deserved it. He had closed two million dollars in sales with many more days left in the month. His margin was at 24%. He was probably out doing who the hell knows what and I wish I had joined him!" thought Gary to himself.

Gary: James took a small break, came back, and went back to work. I am sure he is continuing to push on other deals he has in the pipeline.

The Man: Well, tell him good job from me, but don't be overly thankful. I don't want him requesting more money. Just tell him that I sure wish that $600,000 would have been $650,000.

"It's never enough, is it? You F'er! James is our best sales guy. He deserved thanks for his tireless work and appreciation for what he was doing for the company," is what Gary wanted to say.

Gary: Will do.

It was strange how Gary worked tirelessly for this man but always felt like it was never good enough. He began to learn that these late Friday night impromptu sessions were meant to drive him harder and to make him feel small. He was brainwashed to feel like he had never done enough, had not outwitted the competition fast enough, had not called enough clients, had not put enough orders through, had not managed his people vigorously enough and so on. That was the Man's management style. IT WAS NEVER ENOUGH!

"Enough." The word was shoved out of his lips with an outward gasp. Why did the wheel never seem to stop, or better yet, why wouldn't the Man give him a reprieve for just one breath and maybe, just once, thank him and acknowledge him for what he had done and what he was continuing to do for the company? He had given everything to the Man and his company, and it was not enough, never was. Gary seemed to be on that interminable cycle of Eat, Sleep, Work, and Repeat. The Man lived, breathed, and loved this cycle and seemed to always hint with little jokes and off-handed comments that Gary wasn't doing the ENOUGH!

Gary had been successful at this job despite the insufferable scrutiny from the man that owned the place. The company was just a boutique organization before he started, with most of the prior sales opened and closed by the Man. It had to be the Man because most salespeople would not stay long enough to have even a dimple of an impact on the company's bottom line. It wasn't the job. It wasn't what the company offered. It wasn't even the marketplace. It was the Man. He hired them on and tore them up. To give the Man credit, the under-the-table deals that he engineered kept the lights on and the people who stayed, employed. Gary never asked about the details of those deals because he knew that what he would learn wouldn't be something he could repeat to anyone or implement himself. It wasn't his business any way. It didn't help that the company had a shady reputation either before he came on board. Hey, the Man had to survive! Most industry partners were more scared of the tongue lashing the Man would fire off at them than excited for the opportunity to partner. Nonetheless, they did business with him. They just did it from a safe distance.

Gary was recruited to sell everything and sell everything he did. Sales grew every year. Gary brought an openness to industry partnerships built around collaboration and mutual respect. Relationships marched in parallel with that willingness. Customers, the market, and the competition were beginning to take notice. He gave a polish and benevolence to the place. He brought real sales talent into the organization and shielded them from the Man's narcissistic effervescence. Their corporate credibility began to blossom. Companies of real merit were seeking them out to do business. The same industry partners that avoided the Man, sought out Gary even though most of those meetings were done off-site. The company was maturing and really making a difference. Things were happening and the Man was quietly impressed, not with Gary, but with his own decision to hire Gary.

Before Gary took his first seat in his cubicle at the salt mine, he knew the Man had a reputation. The Man was charismatic, tenacious, and a true salesman. So, metaphors were quickly born out of all the descriptions. He could sell snow to Eskimos and sand to Arabs. He was also like a dog on raw meat. The word "no" actually meant, "Ask for the sale again." The glib charm coupled with the resolute work ethic were driven by a full, high octane tank of greed. He was a bully. But the bully could sell. Gary had never seen anyone as relentless or fast on his feet. The angles the Man would find and execute were jaw dropping. The strategy of getting the Benjamins was unmatched by anyone he had ever seen before. The Man had smarts and allure. He was driven and witty when he wanted to be. He was friendly when he knew there was something in it for him. The Man was a self-driven, persistent, egocentric narcissist.

Before Gary joined, the company had a revolving door of salespeople – in and out they went. Most people who joined, worked for three months, got burnt out and quit. They just couldn't work for a man that never thanked or appreciated them and was never humble. He never let them go home at night thinking that they had done enough. Worst of all, the Man constantly compared everyone's work ethic to his own. They could never live up to that! It was a losing game and if they didn't intrinsically understand the Man – his style, his humor, his way – they found an onramp to the nearest highway they could and never looked back.

Fortunately for Gary, he figured out the Man on day one. It was quite simple. The fastest way to own narcissists is to compliment them and feed their ego. Gary stoked the man's fire. He then combined the three rules to being successful in business, taught to him by his father, with the three rules he learned from the Man on his first day. His dad's philosophy to be successful was straight forward:

- *Rule #1* – Get to work on time.
- *Rule #2* - Don't do personal shit (stuff) on company time.
- *Rule #3* – Do what the boss says.

Those three rules seemed to be so hard for so many others to follow. Gary could never understand that. It seemed like a super simple work equation for success. Gary found the rules natural and, as a result, was successful at every job he had by simply following them. Was it his secret? How could it be a secret if it just seemed so obvious? Gary couldn't understand why people he had worked with could never just follow these three simple rules. Anytime he saw someone fall out of a job, he could draw a direct cause and effect line from failing to follow any or all these rules. It was perplexing. If the rules had been more complicated or involved more steps, Gary might have failed too. He wasn't the smartest guy there was. There were many things he wasn't, but a staunch observer of those three rules compensated for most of his own weaknesses. He combined those three rules with the newly discovered rules he learned from the Man. He articulately termed them the "The Ignore Rules." Pretty catchy right? These were the three new gems he discovered:

- ***Rule #1*** – Ignore the Man's lewd jokes.
- ***Rule #2*** – Ignore the Man's temper.
- ***Rule #3*** – Ignore the Man's narcissism.

And, voila! That was all he had to do and that was all he did. The company, the Man, and Gary all benefitted – here was another pearl that shone through the poop. Gary knew it would take a crazy work ethic to grow an initiative-based boutique sales operation that was initially just "putzing" along. And to be honest, he just didn't know any other way to work. That was just what he did – it was who he was. It didn't matter what it took or how long it took, he was going to do whatever it took and never hesitate. His dedication to the job, and the Man that he grew to loathe, was his driving source. He just gave it all to the business. And it was fun at first.

If you knew the difference between work and play, you were doing something wrong. He was not doing anything wrong. He couldn't tell the difference. Wasn't that what everyone was looking for in a career? It wasn't his business. He knew that, and he didn't care. He was going to treat it like it was his very own and play. That was just how he was hard wired. His drive was a gift he didn't remember ever receiving or working on. Was it from watching his mom and dad work tirelessly in their own business when he was a kid? Was it his own instinct to "just do it"? "Just do it" – like the Nike TV commercials he grew up watching that inspired viewers to face any daunting challenge by sheer force of will, overcome them and succeed. After a while he stopped asking and was quite thankful to have such a natural born motor humming through his veins every workday. The Man loved it and took credit for it. The Man knew he had someone who naturally knew what it took. Hard Work!

The Pearl: While being constantly scrutinized sucks, it can be valuable in sharpening your skills if you are open to it.

- *Rule #1* - Get to work on time
- *Rule #2* - Don't do personal shit on company time
- *Rule# 3* - Do what the boss says.

Mind these three rules and you will be unbeatable and promotable.

3

READY TO FACE THE CHALLENGE...
AND WALK AWAY

Working early. Working late. Working on weekends. Working on personal time. Working all the time became Gary's modus operandi. But Friday! Why the weekly late-night ambush on Friday? The day was done. The week was done, and yet the Man had to come into his office and just do him. The Man thought employees were good if they worked 8 hours a day, better if they did 10 hours, and if they did 12 hours, they were fucking awesome.

Everyone in the place scattered the minute the Man came into Gary's office on Friday evening. They didn't want to face the constant off-color remarks and those glorious boastful stories of the Man's auspicious past. They also didn't want to be told they hadn't done enough again and didn't want to sit through another comedy routine while the Man supplemented his back-handed comments about their performance with tasteless joke after tasteless joke. The Man always took credit for the productivity anyway. He thought he was the driving force and when he was around, 'magic' happened. The sad truth about it was when the Man was in the office, it was stifling. Everyone just felt helpless. Gary gave his crew credit though. They became experts at smiling back at the Man even in their suffocating helplessness. When the Man was away, the people were free to kill it. Gary gave them the freedom to kick ass and build the business. He hired them and trusted them to do what needed to be done. With clear guidance and the power of belief in their abilities, his people did amazing. 'Magic' did indeed happen. They were able to do what they intuitively felt needed to be done without restrictions. They were in tune with their customers, the trends, and the marketplace. They just required support and belief. The freedom from the owner's absence gave them the ability to hustle to tremendous success.

There is a proverb, "When the cat's away, the mice will play". At the salt mine, the mice didn't play, but worked their tails off. They wouldn't dare bruise the confidence they knew Gary had in them. Goofing off was rare when the cat wasn't around. When the cat got back, the freedom that was building the business was snuffed out. People were subjected to the Man's interrogation, constant inspection and the you-never-do-enough comments. His prowling put a stop to the hustle. Gary's people scattered when the cat came sauntering around. It was just too difficult to get anything done. They especially scattered at 5pm on Fridays. Gary used to just laugh at what chickens, or mice, they were. These were fierce hustlers, but when the cat was around, they got squeamish and were the definition of scared little mice. Gary was left to be the bait for the very hungry cat. He didn't have a choice. He had to hunker down, take a deep breath, and welcome the salt mine cat in with a grin, waiting to be eaten.

Gary met the cat nose-to-nose in those impromptu meetings at 4:58pm every Friday. He didn't even think about packing up for the weekend. He knew the cat was prowling and heading for him. He could run, but then he would be a coward. He could act as if he was on the phone when the Man came in, but it would just be avoiding the unavoidable joust. He didn't go through this informal whipping for just a year or two or three. He succumbed to it for decades. Yes, the "decade" had an "s" after it. What the hell was his problem? He asked himself that all the time. He must be a masochist. He never thought he liked pain. He avoided it like snow avoided the Sahara Desert. He wouldn't get near pain if pain was the woman of his dreams. What the hell was keeping him there subjected to the continual crappy leadership, marginalization, and constant scrutiny that would simply pull a curtain over any weekend reprieve? This was the only reality he knew. That was just what a job was everywhere – a massive ordeal dealing with a boss. It was normal to be questioned by a tyrant. It was normal to feel like you were never good enough. It was normal to never be thanked and be marginalized. Or so he thought!

Why was he staying? He had built a revenue machine for the Man. He implemented systems borrowed from best practices he had observed from his competitors and the marketplace. He was making good money. There was so much to be happy, comfortable, and thankful for. Was he staying for his people? Maybe. Was it the money? No! He stayed because he had built the damn place. He was a builder. That should have been his life's job title. He built the engine, hired the people, crafted the strategy, and nailed the contracts, all despite the Man's meddling. But when you got down to it, the real reason he stayed was that he didn't know how to quit. That was the real problem. That was the source of his misery. It wasn't the Man's fault at all. He had to face this challenge – a challenge of his own making that had little to do with his work or the Man. He had to stare in the mirror even if he hated what was staring back at him. It is so easy to just turn away from the mirror, flip the light off and walk away. A lot of people do that. He was doing that. His staying was the fruit of that exercise. It couldn't be the image in the mirror causing all the pain, stress, and drama, could it? Yep, it could! That was the realization that rocked his world. The complaints about the Man were just a distraction from the real problem. "Why couldn't it be something or someone else?" he thought. He had to face the truth, his truth. It was him, nothing but him. It was time to change. It was time to do it differently and it would all begin with an honest to goodness stare down with his own worst enemy – his devil himself. Fuck. That was going to be tough. He couldn't face it. But he had to, and he would realize later that it wasn't as hard or as scary as he thought it would be. The decision to face it was the toughest part. Everything else afterward was just a glide. Like that day he stood ready to jump out of the plane fearing the step out and then realizing that it wasn't such a big leap after all.

He was ready to move out and move on, confident that it wouldn't be as hard as his fears made it.

The Pearl: When you feel like you are constantly being hunted and beat down, try this confidence booster. Stand in front of a mirror, turn the video on your phone, give yourself a five second stare down in the mirror, smile at yourself, and then at the top of your lungs, "I am magnificent!!!" It is guaranteed to send chills up and down your spine and make you smile. Save the video and watch it any time you need it.

4

DON'T QUIT, EVER

A quick Google search renders hundreds of "Don't Quit" inspirational messages. It was obvious why Gary never quit anything. Between his own maniacal, self-induced, masochistic determination and the relentless cultural sledgehammered messages battered to the brain, he did not dare quit. He didn't even think about it. Quotes stigmatizing quitting dominate the wonderful worldwide web. "If you believe in yourself and have dedication and pride - and never quit, you'll be a winner," stated Bear Bryant, the famed Alabama football coach whose don't-quit mentality made him one of the most revered engineers of the game. The message to Gary was clear. A person is a loser if he pushes aside dedication and pride and quits. "Winners never quit, and quitters never win," exclaimed Vince Lombardi, the revolutionary Hall of Fame professional football coach who helped establish the NFL as the premier sport in the United States. Quitters are one hundred and fifty percent losers. You might as well go to bed and suck it if you quit. The fastest way to being successful was this recipe from the greatest heavyweight boxer of all time, Muhammed Ali: "Don't quit. Suffer now and live the rest of your life as a champion." Gary wasn't about to argue with Ali. Who in their right mind would ever do that? That quote was inspirational. And then there was this doozy from former U.S. President Richard Nixon, "Defeat doesn't finish a man, quitting does. A man is not finished when he's defeated. He's finished when he quits." Even an impeached U.S. President believed in. DON'T DO IT!

These and about a thousand other, "Don't You Even Think about Quitting Messages," blared out from the bullhorn to always keep going. Gary knew that the intent of these messages was a good thing, inspiring people to persevere. He needed to believe in himself in the face of any adversity and keep going. In fact, one of the most personal messages Gary leaned on often was another don't quit quote offered by Winston Churchill, the former Prime Minister of the UK who faced down Nazi fascism during World War II: "If you're going through hell, keep going." Gary liked that "don't quit" message so much that he taped it to his computer screen and often offered it to his people when they were confronted with a problem or obstacle. How about that for inspiration. Don't quit, people!

Everyone seemed to have some mantra around not quitting. The Man posted "Don't Quit" messages all over the walls in the salt mine. There were no pictures of a serene scene of nature, or even abstract art. The message was clearly communicated by the Man's taste in wall art, "DON'T QUIT!" There were images of people climbing mountains with no ropes, some guy pushing a boulder up a steep hill, a surfer about to be swallowed up by an 80-foot wave. Gary wouldn't be caught dead climbing a mountain without a rope or pushing a 100-ton boulder up a hill, or even get on a surfboard, but as far as work was concerned, he would never fucking quit. That was a fact.

If the words, pictures, and descriptions on the salt mine walls weren't enough for anyone to develop a massive aversion to the word "quit", examples of people winning in the face of quitting were everywhere. Gary certainly didn't have to look very hard to see living and breathing viral examples of perseverance and victory. Social media was flooded with cases of everyday people kicking ass and taking names every day. Rags to riches stories were like oxygen. And all those comeback wins in sports, succeeding in the face of unbearable and insufferable odds, or those climbs to Everest, Cinderella stories that came from every part of humanity that demonstrated the best of the human spirit to overcome and win. Anybody remember the movie Rocky?

What Gary faced at work wasn't anywhere near those types of challenges. But he was so unhappy with the weight of those messages. He didn't need any of them to be a winner and to continue in any adversarial situation. When Gary thought of all those amazing examples, it gave him hope and put things in perspective. If he applied those examples to his own situation, it could thrust him through his own adversity and onward to winning. He would keep working at a job that was killing him. He would still be miserable, but he would have persevered and won. Yippee!

When was quitting a positive? Well, there were a million examples of those everywhere. Anything related to personal hygiene for one. You better quit that right now. There were millions of dollars to be made in getting you to just quit farting, burping, snoring, and smelling. Bad habits too had to be immediately dropped: smoking, chewing your nails, drinking, and any other personal abnormality that was not socially normal. You better stop and we will sell you the fix for $19.95 and if you buy within the next 5 minutes, we will double the offer and throw in a free set of steak knives. You must quit! You are too fat, too skinny, too bald, too hairy, too tall, and too short. Quit, quit, quit!!! You can become the better you if you just freaking stop being so gross or just being who you are. Don't you even dare try and persevere through your mess of an existence.

There were examples of people who achieved great things, even happiness, by quitting. In fact, most super successful people had started down one road, changed course, and went on to achieve tremendous success. Seemed reasonable enough. Didn't seem like many of these choices were rocket science. Why did Gary treat it so? Who knows? What he did know was that he had to break a habit. He had to change his mentality and quit what he was thinking, doing, and feeling to move on toward a life without the salt mine boss.

As Gary continued to stare at himself in the bathroom mirror, his mind was focused on the meaning of "quitting." The word was beginning to take on a new and more personal form for him. The new perspective would completely alter his future, actions, relationships, and peace. He could embrace the word "quit" and cuddle with it like a child cuddles a teddy bear. He could win and win big because of it. All the cultural and societal judgement wouldn't matter. The peer pressure to never quit would be meaningless. The pressure to quit would take center stage and be featured in the bright lights of the marquee. Losing would be replaced by winning and the fuel to be victorious took the big and bold form of resigning. Quit and win!

Gary knew exactly what his problem was and maybe more importantly, what his problem was not – being honest with himself. He knew it was not the Man. It wasn't the narcissist he was working for. It wasn't the man that once proudly exhorted to him the three key rules to live by in business (much, much different than Gary's own):

Rule #1 – Always wear a tie.

(Gary's interpretation of Rule#1 – I will always own and control you until the day I die.)

Rule #2 – Never Change your logo.

(Gary's interpretation of Rule #2 – I or better yet 'we' will never change. Change is never good and if we had to change, we would have to admit that we were not the best, or that we did something wrong and that is never going to happen.)

(Gary's further interpretation: I am so fucked working for this man.)

Rule #3 – *Cheat on your taxes but never cheat on your spouse.*

(Gary's interpretation of Rule #3 – Morally, I am your God because I can put three rules together in any arrangement and they make sense even if they are thrown together like a dog, cat, and Ferris wheel.)

No, Gary's problem wasn't the Man, it was the fact that he never quit from anything in his life unless the decision to quit was made for him or his physical being screamed, "Listen fucker, you are going to quit because I am putting you in a hospital. I am done with your perseverance horseshit!" His problem was staring right at him like a prize fighter stares down his next heavy weight opponent. This was going to be the biggest fight he had ever faced, and he would be damned if he would get knocked out. He knew that even if he did get his head knocked off the block, he would get back up again and again and again. He was going to reach deep to grab the courage to quit. It was going to take everything he had. The bell had rung. The heavyweight was waiting, licking his proverbial chops, fists clenched, site centered, jab, upper cut, roundhouse, unanimous decision!

The Pearl: There is no shame in quitting. You don't always have to persevere Life doesn't have to be hard and have to be endured to be valuable. If it comes to you easily, then take it and be grateful for it. Quit to win!

5

CHALLENGE VS. OPPORTUNITY

To stop, cease or discontinue. To depart from, to leave. To give up or resign, relinquish. Funny how all those words that define the word "quit," seemed so damn negative. Not one word pointed to continue, win, succeed, or be happy. Gary felt like a loser just reading the words. The description and synonyms of "quit" sounded and even tasted like an unsavory loss and a mouthful of poop. They made the wonderful impression of not having enough perseverance, character, or guts to get through whatever was needed for success. Quitters simply weren't good enough.

"Shift your mindset!" – that was intriguing though. Could that be the way? Gary used an approach that he could apply to his predicament. This was the challenge, or better yet, the opportunity. Quitting wasn't the bad guy; it was a good guy in a bad guy's suit presenting an opportunity. What was causing him so much trouble was that it seemed that the only solution was to utilize the one word not in his vocabulary. He wondered if he could simply change that word "quit" for three new ones: "shift your mindset". Just like he substituted the word "challenge" with the word "opportunity" all the time. Change the situation by changing your thoughts and changing the words that described the problem. Hmmm, this thought had some promise. Change the word(s). Could it be that simple?

When he changed the word, he changed his attitude. He used to remind himself and his salespeople that as they encountered a tough situation, or a challenge, they should always replace the word "challenge" with a different word, "opportunity." Just that slight word modification seemed to transform the perspective, and change the attitude as well as approach, all in a good way. It focused employees on the possibilities instead of the impossibilities. It seemed to put the sights on achievement and getting to a positive result successfully rather than being subjected to an obstacle with a potential bad ending.

To change those three personally terrifying words, "to give up," was, well, not like a Tony Robbins Break Through moment for him, but it was a small fissure in his perspective that would create huge positive change for Gary for the rest of his life. It would smash wide open an understanding that there was a whole new definition of the word "quit" and because of it he would be able to achieve everything in his life that he ever dreamed of. He was filled with possibilities instead of the pathetic glance that greeted him when he first walked into the salt mine bathroom.

The Pearl: Change the word and it changes the attitude and the approach. Take the next thing you are challenged with and rename it opportunity. It is easy to shift the mindset. Now imagine the possibilities.

6

THE SUPER UGLY EXAMPLE

Quitting. It wasn't a word in Gary's vocabulary or a concept that had ever remotely crossed his mind. He couldn't remember if he had ever started anything and quit it before it was done. Gary didn't quit anything even if it was bad for him. Ever sat through a bad movie or read a bad book? Gary did a lot. He knew it was going to be bad from the very start, and yet he was committed to seeing even the worst story to its end. He knew it wouldn't get any better, but he watched and read on anyway. With more and more futile time invested in bad storytelling, he complained about it along the way but never stopped watching the movie or reading the book. He kept hoping for the story to get better. Well, it never did. He was never surprised that the bad start had a bad ending, but he was disappointed anyway. He was disappointed that he just spent time he would never get back hoping for a juicy story with a juicy ending. That summed up where Gary found himself almost every time. Watching the bad movie, reading the bad book and being disappointed badly because it never got better. He knew it wouldn't every time, but he sat through it anyway. He would never quit even though he went through this over and over and over. Yep, that was him!

If Gary thought really hard about it though, he did in fact quit a couple of times in his life. There was the time when he was a newspaper delivery boy. This was at a time when having a newspaper route was the most coveted job for any neighborhood kid. Gary was the kid who had that job. He had the big bike with the baskets that sat like saddle bags on each side of the back wheel that every kid envied. He would stuff those baskets so full of newspapers that he would have a hard time keeping the bike upright as he peddled up and down the neighborhood streets. He would ride around slinging newspapers to every porch. "Porching" was a sign of true skill and demonstrated professionalism and mastery as a newspaper delivery boy. Gary took pride in every throw that safely landed on his customer's porch. He could make about $200 a month if he performed well and that didn't include tips for "porching". Those were big bucks for an eleven-year-old. Newspaper home delivery barely exists anymore. The news is now 24/7 on smart phones, no subscription or pesky newspaper boy required. He worked the job for five years, riding his bike throughout the neighborhood slinging papers from his two-wheeled steed on to every porch of his adoring customers. The five years, apparently, were the longest the newspaper manager said any kid his age had ever worked for them. He took a lot of pride in that. The manager obviously knew how to push the right buttons to keep him working. That simple comment, "Kid, you're the longest working paper boy we have ever had working for us," was all that was needed for the kid to keep on working.

One day, the newspaper announced that they were changing from an afternoon delivery model to a morning one. Competition from the other morning city newspaper was forcing them to go head-to-head with morning delivery to stay in the business. This was going to be a problem for Gary. He had to go to school and there was no way he could wake up at 4:30 am in the morning to get his route done and make it to school every day, especially in the winter. Chances were that if the paper hadn't made the change to morning delivery, Gary would still be "porching" every newspaper from his bike today at the age of 44. Needless to say, Gary's mom made the decision for him. School came first. According to Gary, the newspaper "quit" wasn't his fault. How could he be "blamed" for the resignation? His mother was the real culprit here. His mother!

Gary did quit playing the trumpet when he was 12 years old. He couldn't escape that black mark on his life's résumé. What a chump he was! Yep, it had been his own decision, his own fault. He had quit by his own hand. When Gary was a little boy, he used to listen to Herb Alpert and the Tijuana Brass. He had found an Alpert album rummaging through his dad's old record collection stored under the stairs in his basement. The Tijuana Brass was a jazz-mariachi band from the 1960s and 70s. Man, could they blow. He smiled every time he thought of their rhythm, style, and class. A whole group dedicated to jazzy and funky brass. Alpert made the trumpet cool. He was charismatic, slick, and confident. As Gary looked at one of their album covers with pictures of the band, he, too, dreamed about being charismatic, slick, and confident. So, as the five-year old figured, learning the trumpet was the straightest and fastest way to get on that album cover. Gary played for two years. He practiced and practiced and practiced. By his own estimation, he had mastered the lip buzz pucker that made the sound sing out of the end of the horn. It was a lot of fun. It was loud. It was truly special. He thought it was awesome. His mom and dad, however, had their ears ringing all the time. The dog was completely annoyed. Gary, though, never got that chance to play, the "Lonely Bull" or "The Mexican Shuffle" or "The Spanish Flea." – songs Herb Alpert made come alive. While he loved the music, his musical talent was little to be desired. Gary never came close to playing any of those tunes he grew up with. He had mastered Mary Had a Little Lamb and Twinkle Twinkle Little Star. He rocked those for sure, but that was as far as his pucker would take him. This was one of Gary's biggest disappointments in his young life – quitting the trumpet. He would never make that album cover and travel the world blowing a horn. A true first world problem, but he was just a kid, and this was his dream. Quitting the trumpet was a sad moment. He was never to blow again.

Gary was also a terrible gambler because of the "no quit" problem he had. If he sat down at a blackjack table, he wouldn't leave until he had to. To put it simply, he didn't leave the table until he was out of money. As long as he had money and kept winning or losing, he would keep betting and playing. It wasn't over until his pockets were empty. That is not a good gambling trait if you don't want to go bankrupt. Gary had to quit that altogether. This may have been Gary's first indication that quitting was not always a bad decision.

Gary had never been a witness to anyone quitting except for one super ugly example. Just this one example would change his life completely, but more on that later. His family never gave him a "quit" example to follow. He had no reference that illustrated quitting was doable and that it was NOT the end of the world. Quitting just didn't exist in his world. As someone who was responsible, committed and stayed true to his word and ambitions, quitting was never invited to the party. His parents had always been married, they always had the same job, same friends, same routine, and the same habits. Nothing ever changed. His dad always smoked, and his mom always drank. There was never any life transition where anything had to be stopped, shifted, or left, at least not by his choice. If it wasn't by his choice, it wasn't quitting. Eat, sleep, work, don't quit, and repeat. There was never a witnessed instance when someone had pivoted from what he was doing to positively change a situation by leaving it behind. All he ever saw was commitment and perseverance to a decision and never wavering from it. A commitment to one's word. A commitment to follow through and finish. A commitment to a choice or a decision, except for that super ugly example.

The super ugly example, a simple and innocent offense in intention but malicious in effect, repulsed and disappointed Gary. He made a conscious mental decision to avoid doing the same at all costs. Sometimes, it doesn't take a lot to affect someone so profoundly. Small things could have such a weighty influence on a person's character and future actions. Gary had been an eyewitness to this super ugly example so many times that it reinforced the never quit component in his own DNA. In retrospect, this part of his DNA was a great reason why he had accomplished so much in his life and gained the respect of people around him. He could always be counted on. He had accomplished a lot by keeping on and persevering. People just knew that Gary would always come through. However, he was now realizing that it was also the part of his DNA that was slowly killing him.

Simply put, the super ugly example appeared when someone would commit to doing something great, grand, and magnificent and then not do it. They would set expectations and then bail. They would tell everyone that they were going to take the world by storm and do something revolutionary and important with their own lives. They were going to accomplish something big. They talked about their ambitions with their chin up, shoulder blades pressed back and conviction piercing from their eyes. They were dreaming, pursuing that dream with gusto, sharing that dream with everyone around that would listen and expressing excitement for what lay ahead of them. Hell, everyone loved to be a part of that dream. The dreamers would receive all the kudos and adulation bestowed upon those who expressed they were going to do something big, something important, something that would change their life for the better. Then, they wouldn't do it. It was like being a part of a big, fat smelly and disappointing fart. That was it. They wouldn't even try! These people would get everyone around them so excited and twitter-patted for their grand plan. Unfortunately, the big plan was all just a pipe dream masquerading as an ambition. People would start to gossip about "the plan" and how successful person X would be and what great things were going to be accomplished. That buzz of optimism and hope filled the air. Gary would even get wound up in his friends' and family's ambitious dreams too. The energy it created was infectious. That was a good thing, right? It was awesome to watch someone decide to take great leaps toward something of grandeur. Soon, someone else would catch the dream bug and announce plans to do something awesome too. These inevitably inspired others to outdo associates with plans of their own to be happy, rich, successful, and rule the planet.

Unfortunately, few, if any, ever even started. The grand expectation was popped like a bubble into a fat pile of disappointment. They quit before they even tried. They psyched themselves out and suffered failures that they hadn't even attempted. Every excuse known to mankind was used for why they didn't achieve what they so proudly boasted about. In most cases, they didn't even take the first step, or if they did, the first obstacle, big or small, that cropped up completely crushed that dream. There was no jumping out of that plane. Hell, they didn't even get on the plane in the first place. They just walked past that plane sitting on the tarmac hoping no one would notice that they hadn't even suited up and packed their parachute.

It annoyed Gary beyond the moon. He hated when people said they were going to do something and never followed through. He damn near judged them as liars. He felt like he was more devastated in their failure then they were. This was quitting before starting – the worst sort of quitting. Gary would never do that. The only time, maybe, was if he said he was going to do something and he was incapacitated in some way, like lost an arm, a leg, or his mental capacity. Well, the likelihood of that ever happening was never going to tarnish his words so he would never do that anyway. It was super ugly!

Gary had a friend that announced that he was finally going to start his own business. He had talked about it for years and was finally going to take the jump and pursue his dream. His friend had worked all his life for someone else. His friend knew the business inside and out, and it was only natural that he would kill it as a CEO. Gary slipped into his cheerleading outfit and got his pom-poms only to be cheering on a player again who never took the field. His friend never even quit his job. He miserably worked there to his last day.

Most of the time, Gary sat through these orations of fantastic ambitions from his friends, knowing they would go nowhere. He tempered his enthusiasm and his "hoorays", and became a skeptic over time. This wasn't good either and people began to avoid telling him anything. "He was being too negative," his friends would say. Gary was okay with that because he was tired of being wound up in their dreams only to be left with no one to root for. Maybe it was because they didn't know how to go forward or maybe they were just trying to impress. Nevertheless, Gary could not understand the mentality. It was a black and white issue for him. Why did they even say they were going to do something in the first place? It made them seem like just big talkers in Gary's eyes. He felt bad for judging them, but he had to admit to himself that that was exactly what he was doing – judging. If the reason they didn't go forward was because they didn't know how, Gary had the answer to that issue all day long. He was often required to go forward, not knowing what the first step was. Hell, it happened to him all the time. If he waited to completely know something before he moved forward, he wouldn't have ever gone anywhere. Moving forward in the absence of knowing is essential for accomplishing anything. People just psyched themselves out of doing a lot of things because they just overthink it. Their minds push the plans to places they would probably never go and as a result they would get paralyzed and resign. Their own ambition was too overwhelming. It was the whole out-think, out-believe and out-sabotage one's own plan concept.

There was an incredible ironic twist that serendipitously shot out of this super ugly example that Gary learned, leveraged, and used all the time. It became his supreme calling card. It was the key to him achieving everything he set his mind to. He would never disappoint himself or anyone else who was around him as a result. It was automatic, a little evil, and put a shitload of pressure on him, but it always pushed him to succeed. It always worked.

Here was Gary's great secret in doing anything. Announce to everyone what he was going to do. Much in the same way everyone else did, but Gary followed through. Just by saying it, he had no choice but to do it. People's expectations were raised. There was no way Gary would disappoint or even bruise his word or their expectations. The amount of personal and perceived peer pressure that he put on himself, forced him to do it. Sometimes it was handy to have a self-inflicted whip. This was his motivation – the secret. It was a little painful with an added dash of pressure, but that was the reason why he could always be counted on for his word and his dream pursuits. He would always do what he said. This was a mode of operation that would help him reach the many peaks he was so proud of. It was also the way of life that would eventually put him in the hospital.

Once Gary announced to the world what he was going to do, he went into phase two of his action plan. He did two things:

1) He just went forward despite not knowing how to start or go forward. Any step was a step. It didn't matter how menial or small it may have seemed. How to proceed was easily answered by just doing the first thing that came to mind. It didn't matter if it was the right step at all. It was just important to take the step. That first step would help him determine the next one. Just take the f'ing step without the comfort of knowing if it was in the right direction. The action of the step was what was important. Chances were that what he learned from just attempting the first step would help him take the next step and then before he knew it, he wasn't just stepping anymore, he was leaping forward toward his vision at the speed of light.

2) Like the idiom states, Gary "crossed that bridge when he came to it." Delay worrying about something that might happen until it actually does happen. Cross one bridge at a time. Everything other than the first bridge and the first step was just noise. Tuning the noise out and focusing on the bridge directly

in front of him simplified the approach and made it easy, too easy actually.

When Gary employed this approach, all the noise of the "what if's" disappeared. The overwhelming and paralyzing thoughts about all the bridges down the road were eliminated. Those didn't matter. He would get to those later, maybe. He focused all his attention on looking at what was right before him and just tackled that. He didn't try to anticipate what other bridges would bring because he would deal with those bridge crossings if they ever came across his path. Most of the time they didn't and bridges that he never expected popped up in front of him, but by that time he was so far down the proverbial road, he handled those crossings like a Jedi knight. He may never cross those damn issues, circumstances, events, bridges anyway so having them affect his first step made no sense. Those were Gary's tactics and they worked like a hot knife through butter. His hatred of not following through on commitments and his word gave birth to the secret Gary used to not just dream big but to do big.

What would happen when he told everyone he was going to do something and wavered with a change of heart? That happened to Gary many times, but he refused to change his announced commitments. It cornered him. He just continued and clung to his own words despite his own peril and detriment. His secret weapon had no toleration for a change of heart. His secret weapon betrayed him when that happened. It was a curse and prevented him from giving himself any permission to make any deviations or adjustments when logic was screaming at him to quit. Many times, he got stuck moving forward on a commitment his gut shouted at him to stop. His job situation was making him confront this in a big way.

The Pearl: Try this out. Have the courage to announce your plans to all your friends and family. They will surround you with support. You won't let them down and they will be there when you need help to persevere.

When you don't know what to do, just do the first thing that comes to mind. Maybe the first step is to simply announce your plan.

Cross that bridge when you come to it. Don't paralyze yourself with thoughts of all the bridges you have to cross to get to your goal. One bridge, one step, one goal at a time.

7

NEXT STOP - DISCOMFORT

Gary drove home that Friday evening very late. The road home had been vacated by the daily commuters' hours before and he felt at peace with the easy ride, but he was a bit lonely too. There was no one else out on the road he could share the just-got-worked-to-death look with. He told himself to put two hands on the wheel, stare forward, breathe, turn right, stop, turn left, and get home. The daily autopilot glide back to his family.

His wife was waiting for him, and she knew why he was late, but she was puzzled by his calm demeanor. Why wasn't he upset by facing the late Friday ambush again? Maybe Gary didn't have the customary Friday "you didn't do enough" chat with the Man. "Yahoo!" she thought. Maybe the Man gave him some thanks or kudos. Maybe they just talked about sports, the weather or what was the best tie to wear next Monday. Well, it had been none of that. Gary told her that he, in fact, did have the "you didn't do enough chat" again, but that after the chat, he had this awkward stare down with himself in the bathroom and something shifted in him. The winds were turning his ship around and it was in a direction that offered promise, discomfort, and freedom. Could you ever imagine that discomfort would be something necessary, appealing, and magnificent?

The Pearl: When the uncomfortable is staring you down, don't run from it. It will only make it worse. Go up to it and give it a big hug. It is a teddy bear disguised in a monster suit.

8

THE FREE FALL

Gary's breath shot down deep into his belly and ripped out of his lungs as he leaned out of the plane. He tried to grab onto that breath like a falling man trying to snatch a rope that was his only anchor to safety and comfort. He found nothing. The scream that Gary had been so diligently preparing for didn't even make it to his lips. His heartbeat raced to meet his breath's exit in his throat, and he choked. He was on a free fall to nowhere. "What the fuuuck was he doiiinnngg?" he thought. His body went numb. He couldn't feel a thing. The earsplitting sound of the propellers was quickly replaced by deafness. He couldn't hear anything. While it seemed that his hearing was shutting down permanently, the adrenaline that pounded through his skeleton blew his eyes wide open and time froze. His body revolted against his stupid idea of getting uncomfortable and jumping out of a plane. "What a fucker!" it thought. Coincidentally, his mind was thinking the same thing at that moment.

The wind coming at him was more like a wall. It was a force against his body that he had never experienced before – relentless, enveloping, and smothering. He realized that it was the only thing between him and a loud splat. He imagined euphoria, panic, and peeing his pants and then all of the above at once. It was terrifying. For the first time in Gary's life, he was living and breathing in the moment and that was not by choice this time. What an indescribable feeling being present in the moment was! He wasn't thinking about yesterday and nothing about tomorrow. Actually, he wasn't thinking at all. It was a skydiving lobotomy – his very own nirvana. He was just soaking all of it up in real-time. Life and the earth around him colored with a bright fluorescent highlighter. Everything was vivid.

Was it like this all the time or did it require pushing the mind and body to such extremes to achieve such a presence of mind? Each day just thoughtlessly rolled into the next. Before realizing it, those days turned into decades. So much happens while each day is lost to schedules, routines, monotony, stress, and ambition. What would it take to slow down time? The number of times he just sat and listened to the hum and buzz around him could have been counted on his fingers. When did he just sit and feel his body and watched the world spin around him? Never. He realized he lived a life of distraction. He was in a constant state of distracting himself from the world and the body he inhabited. What a waste! He was always so busy going somewhere that he never stopped to see where he was and what he was walking through. Could he do it? Could he just stop, breathe, and get a chance to be in the moment without jumping out of a plane?

Being several miles away from any familiarity was breathtaking once he calmed himself down. As he began to let fear be whipped away by the crushing wind, sound returned to his ears. The loud rush of wind engulfed him in a blanket knitted in cool. He screamed as an effort to be sure he wasn't just dreaming but heard nothing in return. Fresh air pushed past his choked throat and crisply kissed his lungs. It was so sublime! How fresh the air tasted!

As he dropped at 120mph, he couldn't take his sights off the earth below him. It was hypnotizing. He felt light and out of control. He had to force himself to look to his right and left to get whatever semblance of bearings he could. Gary hadn't felt the instructor on his back for the tandem descent down until just then. He now took comfort that someone other than himself was taking the wheel for this ride down.

Gary realized that he went from having a sheer heart attack while jumping out of the plane to feeling comfortably numb, like a Pink Floyd song. He had no sense of falling. In fact, he just felt the opposite – he was floating. His perception of the ground rushing to meet him didn't even register as he fell free at a clip of 200 feet per second. The instructor turned him to the right, and then to the left. Gary was like a firmly held rag doll controlled by a puppeteer riding on his back. This was getting fun. This was letting go. He had never ever let himself be out of control. This was out of control defined.

The Pearl: Letting go is one of the hardest things to do it can be one of the most rewarding things you can do. Fear and being uncomfortable are the two primary sources stopping you from letting go.

Write down your fears and what is making you uncomfortable. Now write down mini steps that can move you forward to letting go that will help diminish your fear and get comfortable with the comfortable.

9

SHARED IDENTITY

The Man was better to Gary than the rest of the miners that worked in the salt mine. The Man liked that Gary would "think" and had initiative. He liked that Gary could take his tasteless jokes and just chuckle without judgement. He liked that he could share his prejudice and sexism without any comment or condemnation. Gary knew who the Man was and there was no changing his stripes. While Gary hated every joke and every bigoted and sexist comment, he just smiled back. This was not a battle worth fighting nor one that could ever be won. Why waste the time or the breath trying? Some subjects like religion, politics, bigotry, sexism, whether a tomato was a fruit or a vegetable, whether dogs were better pets than cats, just weren't worth touching. The Man would never change regardless of the sound logic or morality presented to him. Gary just smiled and moved on. He would let his own actions speak against it all.

Turning the other cheek unfortunately resulted in the Man thinking Gary was a lot like himself. Oh, how wrong he was! Gary was just really good at impersonating a chameleon. It was a characteristic that also made him a very effective salesperson. He could adapt to almost anything when he had to and when it came to the Man's comments and jokes, he had to.

Gary learned what he could from the Man and unlearned the things he was forced to choke down in one of the many late night "mentoring" sessions. Gary was the guy – the Man's chosen one. He was responsible and had the work ethic to finally grow the business the Man so much desired and was unable to do himself. Gary strangely understood the Man. The Man had some redeeming qualities behind the narcissism, sexism, and bigotry. He was loyal. He was that guy you wanted in the foxhole alongside you in the face of overwhelming adversity. The Man was steady, confident and a leader. With that said, Gary was going to deliver what the Man wanted – a growing and stable business that would finally give the Man the legitimacy at the country club. He was going to have to ignore the Man's old school ways. That would prove to be a monumental challenge, or rather, opportunity. The Man was the business's own worst dysfunctional enemy, although he was convinced that he was the business's best asset.

Without a shared identity with a boss, coworker, spouse, friend, neighbor, family member, or partner, communication to get to that common understanding is challenging and working effectively together never works. Without a unified understanding and agreement of where to go and how to get there, no progress is made. Cutting ties and moving on to somewhere or someone that shares vision is the only solution. Remaining in a battle of opinions will create a crisis that will begin to take on a life of its own and just flat out destroy ambition, plans and relationships.

We have all differed in our opinions. When working with someone who is set in their ways but reasonable in their perspective, conflict, discourse, and debate can be very beneficial. Gary was a proponent of a healthy debate. It just made your approach sounder and sharper. It considered all angles. Strategies that value all perspectives foster tremendous goal achievement and shared understanding and respect. But working with inflexible authoritarians requires one-sided compromise, resigning to the other party's beliefs, or quitting and walking away. I am a strong proponent of the later. Gary was a strong proponent of the former and then just stewed in his own resentment sauce.

It all starts with assumptions. The grand word that everyone knows to avoid because even within its spelling disaster lurks. Ass-u-me – when you assume, you make an ASS out of U and Me. Everyone knows this little feature of this word, but we still make assumptions about what someone else wants every minute of every day. Everyone knows not to assume, and the damn word even spells out the error in doing so. But how could Gary solve not being on the same page, not having a shared identity with the Man?

He asked five simple questions. What did he want? What didn't he want? Why did he want it? How did he want it? When did he want it? He didn't make it more complex than that. He stuck to those five "W" questions, and he found out quickly if he had a shared identity of what to do and what was expected, or if he would ever have a shared identity, or if he should just run for the door with a "See ya, wouldn't want to be ya," proclamation.

Gary knew that many people were so passionate about what they believed in that those passions led them to great success. Passions have taken people, relationships and businesses to heights that were never imagined. The belief that fuels that passion can be a transformative demonstration of greatness. However, the other side of the belief sword is just as sharp and equally powerful in a destructive way. Gary tried to stay away from that side of the sword but knew that he contributed his own share of relationship friction in the salt mine. Uncompromising belief creates dysfunction. Egos rise and people believe so strongly in something that they become it. They live it and breathe it. The Man was a poster child of this. By itself, this can be pretty awesome. Thoughts become things. Thoughts become actions. Actions become results. Dreams are achieved. Goals are realized. It's all about the law of attraction. However, there is another side of this and that is where the trouble started with the Man. Gary's boss was becoming a major dick because of his strong uncompromising beliefs. Cooperation, shared identity, teamwork, and success doomed

Gary. Trying to work with such a person was comprehensibly fucked!

Gary was one of those poor, unfortunate idiots subjected to such a person. He tried to change this person for decades. Was he just plain stupid for trying or was he just stubborn? Was his ego not allowing him to walk away? Maybe all of those were true but what was most certainly "dead on" was that it was just another situation where Gary's no-quit attitude would not allow him to scuttle the situation he was in. It would have been so much easier on him and everyone around if he would have just quit. He could have moved on by now.

Gary's no-quit attitude and the Man's inexorable ways built a beautiful monument to the dysfunction god. They fought and yelled at each other constantly. If it weren't for the mutual respect and trust they had between themselves, the relationship would have ended as quickly as a man standing on the gallows waiting for the trap door to fly open. It was so difficult to work with someone who didn't have the same shared identity. There was no way to move that person to a compromise or a common point on the corporate growth horizon. The Man did not compromise! He never changed and he was always right. How did Gary work with a man like that? The only time the Man would compromise was if he got something else in return and that something else was usually such a painful concession in its own right that the original compromise fell to the ground like fine china dropped from a 100-story building. But because of

Gary's awareness of the dysfunction and the notion of a misaligned shared identity, he was able to maneuver like a guppy swimming in between a bunch of hungry sharks.

Shared identity is being on the same page lockstep with each other. It is moving to the same point on the horizon together. It was never going to happen. Both he and the Man wanted a spot on the horizon that represented growth, success, and wealth. Unfortunately, for the both of them, that spot on the horizon was really located at two completely different points in the distance. Yes, the point symbolized the goal and the future, but they weren't on the same spot, and they were apart enough from each other that getting there would prove difficult, if not impossible. Imagine two quarter horses tied to a wagon and both horses moving forward but one pulling left and one pulling right. It was a constant strain and a game of tug of war but moving in the right direction. However, they weren't going anywhere fast. Growth was slow as a result, but they did grow. They did build a solid and financially profitable business although many companies that shared the same business profile were hundreds of employees and hundreds of millions of dollars farther down the road. Every day of fighting the "what" and the "how" took its toll on their relationship. Who was right? Well, they each thought they were. Who was wrong? Well, they each thought the other was. Gary would compromise. He had to in order to survive. It wasn't his company at the end of the day. He was asked to implement tactics and strategies that had no chance from the start. The Man wouldn't listen to him. That stung. He had to implement a strategy knowing it was going to fail from the first step. Moving forward on an action plan, knowing full well it was going to fail but having to go through the process anyway was difficult and demoralizing. It was a complete waste of time and effort that only resulted in inevitable failure. It killed Gary inside.

Even if he didn't believe in the plan and knew full well it was going to fail, Gary gave it his all. That was the only gear he knew. To add salt to the wound, when it did fail, Gary was blamed. It could never be the Man's fault. The only way he could prove they were wrong initiatives and bad ideas was to fail without sabotaging the result. Sabotaging would not prove that the initiative was a bad one and would Gary's integrity call into question. How would he live with that? He didn't know how to fail, and he would not fail on purpose to prove any point. What he knew was that he had to implement these flawed initiatives, give his hundred percent effort, look like a nut job to everyone else who also knew it would fail, and then fail. Then, he would also have to take the blame. That was the equation. Gary would invest extensive time and effort on the Man's initiatives, knowing they were going to be one big fat colossal flop. Ironically, this compromise came at a great reward to Gary – a pearl in the poop.

Here's the reward. The failure of these doomed plans taught him more than he would ever imagine. Yes, he learned bitterness and resentment, but that wasn't the unexpected lessons that would prove to be so appreciated later in his career. No one likes to be around bitter people and learning how to be one would make him the most popular person to not be around. A kill pill in a sales profession for sure. Learning how to bounce the bitterness and the resentment out of his life was the skill he mastered from these failures. Three simple images and a quick mantra expelled the bitter pill:

- *Firstly*, an image of a feather. A reminder to stay light in the face of any adversity.
- *Secondly*, a picture of a pair of scissors cutting a cord. Being tethered to a crappy outcome, event, memory, or action did not serve him, and he couldn't move forward being paralyzed to the past. Learn from it, cut it, and move on.
- *Thirdly*, a grand sweeping image of a highway leading into a grand and picturesque valley. It was a reminder that the future would not be made powerless by the past and to keep moving forward even if it was an inch at a time.

That is how he would move on and then he would cap those images off with a "Fuck bitterness and resentment. They don't serve me, and I don't have time for it. Thanks for the lesson but no thanks to the residue left behind."

Gary knew that this was all about the Man's, "cover your ass," mentality. It pissed him off, quite frankly. Effective leadership is done through actions and not words. Sure, leaders can use words sprinkled in with a little charisma and get anyone to do just about anything, but if they want to lead with integrity, they cannot use those words to point the finger at someone else, even if that someone else was a maniacal boss who garnered no respect. It had nothing to do with showing an executive management unified front either. At the end of the day, Gary had to take responsibility to be accountable for the unwritten items not listed in the job description he accepted when he took on the role to lead. It came with the territory and if he didn't like to point the blame upward, he should not have taken the job in the first place. It didn't matter that the Man didn't want to be accountable for his bad ideas. He was the Man and his narcissism always protected him and never made him wrong. The Man demanded that the failures stop at Gary's feet, and that the wins keep inflating his soaring ego. That was the "bene" that he got as owner of the joint.

After Gary resentfully kicked it around a bit, he let all failures land at his big toes with no transparency that blamed the rightful culprit. In the end, it meant that Gary owned up to it all and that was where it all had to be. After he got over his own self-pity injustice party, he knew that, in the end, it didn't matter to him. He would flip those failures into big learning lessons and big wins to come. It was all about what he did with the loss that mattered and not about who was pinned with the loss that made any difference. It made him tough and refined skills he never knew he needed refined. In the long run, everyone discovered what Gary had kept close to the vest. The fact that Gary accepted the losses like he did gained him immeasurable respect from his people.

The Pearl: Find your mantra. Repeat it until you believe it, then attract it.

Being on the same page with whomever you are with personally or professional seems to be so obvious, but it very rarely occurs unless you are absolutely honest with your "what's," "when's," "how's," and "why's." Get clear on what is driving your actions. Make sure they match up with your counterpart. Get on the same page and go get it!

10

GROWTH IN THE FACE OF "NO"

Imagine working in the type of environment where every step taken was a step scrutinized. It was inescapable. The Man's first response to almost everything he was approached with was an undeniable and resounding, "No." It didn't matter what was asked or presented. The Man's supreme power was built in those two letters. He loved those two letters. He bathed in them, flossed his teeth with them, wiped his butt with them and ultimately wrapped himself up in a fluffy and cuddly NO blanket that shielded him from having to give up any control. "No" was the decisive governor. He would suffocate everyone who worked for him in that blanket. It made him feel like God.

The constant rejections did two things to Gary:

1) He was never comfortable at the head of the sales division of the salt mine because the constant "no" seemed to question all his decision making. He didn't feel empowered to just make the necessary decision and it kind of rocked his confidence. Was he not trusted? Didn't his accomplishments stand for themselves and prove to the Man that his approach to the business was not only sound but also outstanding? He thought that the results from his efforts would give him the credibility for an occasional "yes." Nope. A "yes" could never happen without a complete cavity search. The Man had to put his stamp of approval on everything even if it was a decision to change the two-ply toilet paper to one-ply toilet paper in the interest of fiduciary responsibility.

2) He had to become an incredible and cunning strategist to get all those "no(s)" turned into "yes(es)". Scrutiny causes some to sink and others to fly. Gary chose to fly. The challenge of being constantly scrutinized and told "no" was the opportunity to get good, get better, and be the best. This was the pearl that he picked out of the poop.

The Man administered a form of control that employed a tool for him to feel relevant. Deep down the Man knew that he was not keeping up with anything in the industry and was employing outdated ways, and he really had little he could contribute. The "no" gave him power to counteract the growing insecurities he had around his relevancy in the business.

The upwardly pulsating growth on the company's heart rate monitor was directly connected to Gary's efforts from the first day he started. The time it took to get to the "yeses" created exhaustion, but Gary's efforts beat on daily. With that strong heartbeat, the success of the company marched steadily onward to a promising future. Industry partners were not only actively reaching out to the company, but they were bringing business with them for Gary to consider. Companies weren't just stopping by and running at the sight of the "scrutinizer;" they were staying and strategizing. It was becoming a welcoming place for collaboration. The turnstile that ushered people into the salt mine and rapidly spun them out, stopped turning so quickly. People stayed. People were led. People succeeded. Success attracted incredible talent and Gary was keenly aware of the types of people that would not only be happy working at the salt mine but would also thrive there. He looked for people who cared, were personally inspired by opportunity, and had ambitions. Gary recognized that if they were going to give 8-10 hours of their life daily that they would never get back working at this place, then it better damn well mean something. It was Gary's obligation to them to make it mean something. Life is finite and asking others to spend those precious minutes to make someone else money is a big ask if the work is not meaningful. Gary looked at his own personal weaknesses and hired people that counter-matched those weaknesses with their own strengths. The team took shape and was a well-rounded group of incredible people creating terrific things. Each member felt personally responsible for the company's success. They were empowered. The place was becoming Gary's place in the face of "no."

The Pearl: Get comfortable with NO. Instead of avoiding it, run to it. Sounds stupid but do it. Run to NO.

When you make friends with rejections, you take the fear out of it. For every NO, you are one step closer to YES and one step SMARTER. Going after NO also means you are attracting the UNCOMFORTABLE. You grow every time you do that.

---

15 MINUTE MANIFESTO

Well, you have heard enough about Gary's boss's management style. It was just flat out old-school, and that school had some value for sure, but mostly it didn't. It felt like riding a bike to the moon. It just did not work. It hampered growth, drove people away and only allowed for a select few, the masochists in the crew, to survive. Gary came to be strangely thankful for the Man's management style because it was so different from his own. There was supreme value in contrast. He was able to compare and measure up his own style and tweak on the fly because he had such a stark example to gauge it by. Both management styles were dysfunctional-ly residing in the same operation and that was not healthy. Was Gary being insubordinate by following his own instinctual management style rather than buying in to the Man's dictatorship? Probably. But great value was being born out of the dysfunction. Without its presence, Gary would not have focused on doing things so differently and developing best practices from a meshing of the two styles. The lessons learned on what not to do were very important. Contrasting something in its relative form was the best way to learn and develop strategies that really made a difference. This was the pearl out of the poop.

Gary always mandated that his people took time to read something every day. Just 15 minutes a day would be all that he required. He wanted\them to look at their goals and ambitions, their weaknesses and at what made them feel uncomfortable, find a book, magazine article, blog, or other resource and read or learn about it. Spending those 15 minutes a day digging into these areas would turn into about 7 hours a month of focusing on getting better and getting comfortable with the uncomfortable. How many people do you know that spend 7 hours a month, let alone even 15 minutes a week developing and improving themselves? Few people spend that amount of personal time focusing on sharpening themselves. They couldn't imagine the competitive advantage they would acquire by implementing that 15-minute look in the mirror strategy. Gary could, and he knew that it would not only make his organization very tough to beat, but he would also be giving his people an advantage they would benefit from in business and in their own personal lives. He felt obligated to make those 8-10-hour workdays mean something. Getting comfortable with the uncomfortable was the absolute key to personal growth and just killing it in business. They would have to give him a report or mini presentation at the end of each month. If they didn't spend the 15 minutes a day diving into their own issues, he would simply put them on probation. This was important stuff and he felt it was his duty to help his people develop. He wanted them to be better at the end of the day than when it started. It was his obligation in exchange for the time they were giving him helping the company move toward corporate objectives.

The best salespeople were not just born like the adage says. The masters learned all the time and took the time to refine, refine,

refine. If everyone would just take a break from their busy day and just learn something, their skills would literally explode. Their personal and professional growth would surpass the skills and expertise of their competition because their competition wouldn't be investing in themselves this way. Gary always stayed in the state of a student. When he was, he was humbled and thankful for the lessons out there and maintained an open mind to becoming better every day.

The Pearl: Spending 15 minutes a day on either something you want to pursue, something you want to get better at, or something you want to get more comfortable with, will pay BIG personal dividends. Target something out at the beginning of the month that you want to get better at or more comfortable with. Set a timer for 15 minutes a day, same time every day, and study it. Keep a pig-headed discipline to that one time a day for 15 minutes and go get your goals.

12

WARM INTERLUDE

One Friday evening, the Man came into Gary's office to have the usual talk. The discussion began to center around Gary's concern about competition and the company's ability to keep up with new developments in the marketplace. He knew the Man was strategic, but his ego was so much in the way of his vision, that it didn't seem he could see at all. Often, Gary thought he was the only one paying attention. He felt a little bit crazy. He would talk about upcoming opportunities and lurking threats all the time with the Man. The Man not only didn't see them, but he also didn't care to either. It didn't matter. When a person believes he is the best, nothing else matters to him and threats are perceived to be so far back in the rearview mirror they could never catch up. Gary could not understand that. He felt like a madman waving a neon sign about an oncoming business tsunami, while the Man just laid in the sun not worried about the approaching wave.

"You know what your problem is, Gary? You have an inferiority complex," the Man said.

Gary looked back at him in astonishment. "What? Me? I have an inferiority complex?"

"You don't think you are the best," the Man said with a little smirk of egotism. "When you are the best, nothing else matters."

Gary looked at the Man, took a breath in and exhaled with a calm response. "There was one word that did matter."

"What?" the Man responded with his own confused disbelief.

"Better. The one word was 'better." Better beats best all day long every day. Better recognizes that best can be beaten because of arrogance. There was always someone trying to do better and knock the best off the top of the hill. If you weren't careful in paying attention to better, you would soon be out of business," Gary said.

"Like I said Gary, you have an inferiority complex," the Man extolled.

Incredulously, Gary looked at the Man. It was a nice cutting comment. When Gary heard this, he didn't take it personally at all. The Man had labeled him worse over the years. What scared him the most was how oblivious the Man was and that he was relying on this man to lead the company forward in a very competitive and constantly changing business environment. If the Man was going to sit high atop his ego and not recognize or be concerned with "better" coming fast in the rearview mirror because of his, "I am the best" attitude, the company was doomed. Gary was doomed. The people he led were doomed. Gary should have quit right then and there with that realization, but did he? Hell, no! Dumb. Dumb. Dumb!

The Pearl: Better beats best all day long. If you get too cocky about being the best, watch out, better is coming. Believe in yourself but always know that you can always learn from better. Don't let your ego fool you right out of being in first place.

13

INSPIRATION VS. INTIMIDATION

Gary, read something somewhere about leadership that struck such a cord with him that it became his primary means of leading people. He wished he had come up with it himself, but he was sure he didn't. He gleaned this breakthrough from his very own 15 minute a day exercise he made his people perform. In one of these quarter hour sessions, he read about management and leadership. Up until that time, he was solely subjected to the leadership courses the Man taught every day. If Gary wasn't careful, he would soon become a mini version of the Man. The 15 minute a day idea came from this exact situation. He had to go outside of the organization and get his own identity and perspective. If he didn't, he knew that when he looked into the mirror, it would be the Man staring right back at him and that was no recipe for success. It would have been the tasty recipe for professional sabotage. He wouldn't allow himself to become the monster he worked for. He knew the daily lessons he was getting from the Man and the myopic view it provided was not going to help him develop his skills, lead people, or operate the salt mine. He didn't need any more lessons in the Man's approach. Ironically enough, he was thankful for the doctorate he was acquiring from the Man's model. The Man's lessons offered a real contrast to how things should be done. Without the contrast, Gary thought, he would not really understand precisely how effective alternative leadership and best practices he was reading about could be. Gary's chief professor was not the Man but the 15-Minute Manifesto. The hundreds of books, blinks, podcasts, blogs, and articles he read from the hundreds of leadership and management gurus around the world brought together diverse perspectives. Connecting with these perspectives helped Gary shape his own style.

These resources emphasized what leadership was NOT about. Firstly, effective leadership could never be about ego and narcissism. Wearing ego blinders shuts down the contributions of others and protects the egotist from necessary constructive criticism that would otherwise make him better. Cockiness only opens the door for any competitor's "better" to out-perform you. Being cocky is self-destructive.

A "my way or the highway" mentality and leadership by intimidation techniques never considers other developments, inputs, outputs, or circumstances that come up along the way.

It's kind of like heading down a river and denying the reality of the changing flow, speed, and turbulence of the water's path. The complete delusion that only smooth waters are ahead results in shock when the rapids hit and there is no paddle. Shit! A lot of leaders establish a vision and goal to achieve but the ones that were open to pivoting on their way to those goals achieved monumental success and developed trust within the team they were leading. Contribution from each member on a team is important even if that contribution is just voicing an opinion. People liked to be heard. It is not always necessary to act upon someone's opinion, but they should at least be given the consideration to be heard, and that is leadership.

Snappy back-handed passive-aggressive compliments in the form of jokes are out of the question as well. Yes, this one is super obvious, but it is not uncommon for employees to be subjected to them and pissed off by them. But if that is the case, why do these comments always happen? That's pretty obvious, actually. They are done to reaffirm the pecking order. Leaders use these comments and affirmations every day and in every industry. For example, when the boss doesn't speak the truth openly to sabotage your plan behind your back. They are the boss, and it isn't a plan unless the boss takes your idea, modifies it just enough for it to be called his and not yours. That is a fun one! Or they appear sweet as a candy cane while you are giving a presentation on how you are proposing to take over the planet, then turn indignant because they didn't think of it, get angry, and try to undermine your plan when you step outside to go to the bathroom. These two-bit leaders put people down in a way that is just heinous because if they didn't, they wouldn't feel like they have added value. Yep, that is true. Instead of leading through the "Re's" – redirecting from acquiring additional perspectives, resyncing to be sure that everyone still has a shared identity on what is to be achieved, reexamining to fool proof the plan – they use the "re" that a passive aggressive prick employs, "resentful". And it makes them feel so good!

While Gary's boss would never admit it, this passive aggressive prick knew exactly what he was doing and Gary was stuck getting "done" by the Man's smile-in-his-face, stab-him-in-the-back management style. Gary wanted to scream, cry, hit something, quit but he didn't. The ego-maniacal top dog on the pecking order reaffirmed his position daily. Why? Because privately when he was by himself behind closed doors, the Man knew he was way over his head.

Not providing genuine thanks and gratitude is also one of those management styles that is alive and well in today's salt mines. Sometimes, someone's work is just taken for granted. "Why would I thank them? That was their job? You don't thank someone for doing their jobs!" Gary never got thanked at the salt mine. Well, that is a little bit of a lie. He employed his own passive aggressive tactic to force the Man into a thank you. Yes, it was cheap and cowardly. It didn't feel great that he got one out of him, and it didn't really land on him meaningfully when it happened. It kind of felt as satisfying as a one-night stand or eating a chocolate chip cookie. Tasted good at the time but left him unsatisfied once it left his tongue and travelled down toward his bowels. Getting the Man to say, "thank you" seemed more like an opportunity to manipulate the grand master dragon. Objective accomplished!

How did Gary do it? He brought the Man a cup of coffee. The Man didn't have a choice, did he? Gary smiled as he walked away. Thanks. Such a great word. Besides "hi", "bye" and "please", it was one of the first words taught when learning a new language. Coincidence? No way. Gary used it all the time at the salt mine. He didn't want anything that was done by his people or the company's partners to go unnoticed. It didn't matter if it was their job or not. "Thank you" was an easy way to positively recognize people for doing their jobs well and encourage them to continue. Leaders who do not thank their people feel that to do so would be to give up their insecurely maintained power. They view "thank you" like "sorry". Well, if the Man had to say thank you or sorry, he was admitting he needed someone else, he couldn't have done it without them, he made a mistake or didn't know better. That was not leadership. A leader was strong, flexible, humble, and independent. As long as people are put into leadership roles that they feel insecure about, there will always be little generals making salt mine workers' lives miserable. (With all due respect to Generals, in general).

The general, or rather, the Man, who hovered over Gary's salt mine existence embodied the "NOTs" in leadership. He never admitted he was ever wrong and was never humble. Those characteristics were best for tree-hugging sissy liberals. They had no place in his business. The passive aggressive, no gratitude, myopic, "take it or leave it" control style resembled bullying more than leadership, Gary thought. Gary felt like he had a front row seat with a hot dog, ice cold beer and full bag of popcorn in his hand for that parade every day. Leadership was not about a top to bottom organizational structure where the top issued out-of-touch directives, reprimands, conceit, or marginalization or gave everyone who didn't meet the mysterious job expectations the cold shoulder. Gary's boss never sought out advice because he knew it all and could not understand why Gary always tried to learn new and better ways to lead. He had an inferiority complex!

What Gary new instinctively was that leadership was about compromise, being thankful, creating a bottom-up organizational structure where he supported his people and gave them a clear point on the horizon to move toward together every day. It was not about group hugging here. It was about embracing dysfunction. It was about inspiration versus intimidation. It was all about demonstrating, as a leader, that he truly and genuinely believed in the people that worked for him more than they believed in themselves. Have you ever worked for someone that believed in you more than you believed in yourself? You would never let them down. You did not want to break their incredible perception of you. This was inspiration. Maybe the reason why leaders intimidate rather than inspire is that it is just easier. Do what the Man says and shut up. What kind of bosses have you had? Time to consider a new one if it is currently the latter.

Gary remembered many times in his life where he had a boss, a professor, a mentor, who believed in him more than he believed in himself. He thought that he was pulling one over on these people. How could they think that he was actually that good? Were they nuts? Were they high? "Well I'd be damned if I would ever disappoint them and tarnish their perception of me. Never going to happen. I will work at 100% to maintain their belief in me," is what Gary would tell himself. He operated with his people in the same manner. The Man's style was a stark contrast to Gary's. The Man's "never do enough" style versus, "we can get better because you rock" style clashed and clashed big. It was inspiration versus intimidation at its best. The Man would never inspire his people that way. That would make him vulnerable and not the smartest guy in the room as he always thought himself to be. Gary was not trying to undermine him. He was just trying to get his people to be inspired and believe in themselves as he believed in them the day he hired them. What was wrong with making his people feel that they were vitally important to everything? What was wrong with driving them to make decisions based on "**happy**"? (Another one of Gary's secret management techniques).

The Pearl: If you want to lead people, lead with inspiration. Sure, being authoritarian, uncompromising, and intimidating is easier but to set yourself apart from all the other bad leaders out there and be loved by the people that report to you is extraordinary. Believe in them more than they believe in themselves, and you will not only inspire them to do better than they could imagine but also give them a gift that they will carry with them for the rest of their lives – a memory that you rocked as a leader and a human being.

When you are stuck and don't know what to do, go to **happiness**. Sounds easy and selfish but it is the most selfless decision you can make.

This infuriated the Man. The Man felt like this approach would take away all advantage. If he lost all his leverage, he would lose control, and if he lost control, what else would the Man do but go play checkers every day. He couldn't have that! Never let them feel too important. Never let them ever be too thanked. If you did that, you were soft. If you were too soft, no one would do any work. What was this? The Army? Sorry, effective, and highly productive business organizations cannot work based on fear. They have to work based on belief. A belief in themselves. A belief that what they are doing matters. A belief that what they are doing is making a difference. A belief that they are magnificent and a belief that their boss truly respected their efforts, skills, and time. You do that and you have a rock star operation!

14

SUGAR

Leadership, to Gary, was also making sure that there was a clearly defined singular point on the horizon that he and his team collectively moved toward. There could be no ambiguity when it came to the goal. The Man's singular point on the horizon was always, undeniably revenue growth. Revenue growth was certainly a reasonable goal, especially in a for-profit salt mine like the one Gary worked in, but as a goal by itself, it was hollow, and as nutritious as eating a packet of sugar. This was another example where the divide between Gary's goal setting and the Man's goals created major dysfunction.

The Man's revenue number was not determined by the merit of the business or economics; he would just take the number achieved the previous year and add 20 percent. Viola! Instant goal! There was little discussion on the answers to the questions that had to be answered to put a real plan and a real goal in place. That would take too much time and incorporate introspection. There was no time for that. In addition, if you were always doing it right, as seen in the Man's own eyes, time spent to plan was just a formality and a waste of time. Strategic planning was a psychology session, and the Man was not going to be corporately analyzed. He knew it all. Nothing else mattered.

Gary's focus on growth was based on continued strength and sustainability rather that the attraction to a number – the quick energy rush, temporary happy then crash of a sugar diet. For Gary, revenue (sugar) was going to be the by-product of substance (protein). So, Gary, took the number the Man gave him, 20 percent higher than last year's, and got busy with his team. Gary did not implement a complicated goal-building strategy here. He knew that the more complicated and complex a plan was, the sooner the plan would be abandoned. The plan had to acknowledge human nature and be real.

So, Gary relied on a basic formula and kept it simple. He was into simple. The plan had 6 steps that focused on What, Why, When, How and Where. It was familiar and easy to do.

The Pearl: One step at a time keeps it simple. When you focus on the **one** step right in front of you, you avoid being paralyzed by all the steps you have to take to get where you want to go.

15

THE PLAN

Step One: What (Part I)

Revenue growth should always be a byproduct of "What do we want" initiatives, relationships, and activities in the business. That was the first question he would ask the team. There were a lot of answers to that question. It could be entering a new market, incorporating a newly built enterprise, introducing a new product in a current market, or employing a tactic to guard against competition. There were a lot of answers to the first "what" question and those answers would be thrown up on a board, studied, discussed, debated, and decided. The answers to the "What" (Part I) questions would create the 20 percent revenue growth the Man demanded.

He did not pose the "what" question as it related to vision. A lot of gurus suggested that in the beginning stages of planning, it is helpful to envision what the end line looks like. What does success look like after reaching a goal? What would it mean to the business and employees if the goal is met and so on? Olympians have made this strategy famous and how could he argue with that approach? It often led to incredible success and sometimes even medals. But for Gary, while he understood there was value in visualizing crossing the finish line, at the point of strategic planning, he just felt like it was fantasizing and group hugging. He would implement strategies to help his team gain emotional buy-in later. The initial planning session, while set up simply, was hard work, and he wanted them to focus on answers to the questions before them rather than high fiving one another about how it was going to feel once they hit that magic 20 percent.

Step Two: What (Part II)

Now that the group had debated and agreed to the answers to "What" (Part I), it was time to answer the other part of the "what" that was often forgotten in planning sessions. This "What" was critical to the strategic exercise and gave a context and the contrast to "What" (Part I). The team couldn't have what they wanted without determining and voicing what they didn't want. Debating about what they didn't want was so critical to making sure that the "what" they wanted was legitimate.

It was a litmus test. Not only did it reinforce the "what" they just decided upon achieving, it then forced them to pivot their perspective from the desirable to the undesirable things they wanted to avoid. It spelled out clearly what everyone should avoid. Sure, they could jump over and hop by any obstacle, but if they identified those obstacles before they even started, it was not a matter of exerting any effort to miss them because they would eliminate them before they even started. Identifying what they didn't want also helped them keep everyone honest and kept score of how their progress to what they wanted was coming along. "What" (Part II) was the yang to "What" (Part I)'s yin. Contrary forces that were interrelated, complementary, interconnected, and interdependent to build a comprehensive goal encompassing the positive in ambition with the negative of distractions.

Step Three: Why

"What" questions and the answers that come with them are completely worthless without the "why". "Why" brought the context and meaning to the reasons "what" was important. If you couldn't focus on the reasons for doing something and getting everyone in agreement on those reasons, then you might as well just take the day off. Affix "why" to any question that supports or does not support the "what" and you have the makings and foundations for a plan to achieve whatever goals the "what" determines.

Step Four: How

Like "what" needs the "why" to have meaning, "why" needs the "how" to get going. This is one of the hardest questions to answer. You almost have to make yourself into a mad scientist throwing up theories and hypotheses to figure out the most efficient, cost effective and beneficial modus operandi to implement. Gary made his team break away into multiple mini teams at this moment. He told them to go off by themselves for 30 minutes (not a second more) and brainstorm all the "hows" that came to mind by themselves. He did not want each of his team members to be influenced by anyone else. He wanted their raw approach to "how" without prejudice, judgement, or any other input. He was strict on the time because he wanted unadulterated urgency from the gut. This was a gut check in its primal form. Leave the brain behind for this half hour. What were their instincts? That was how the "how" would be determined. He would bring them all together, mash all the "hows" up and create the tip of the spear to satisfy the "why" and accomplish the "what."

Step Five: When

None of the "what's", "why's" and "how's" mattered without a strong "when." You had to know when it was time to start, readjust, reexamine, redirect, resync, and double-down and when it was time to finish – the deadline. The plan moved and turned because of it. "When" sped-up or slowed down the organization's activities and for some uncanny reason, people operated subconsciously right up to the very last minute of the "when". An over ambitious "when" always sabotaged the "what". Miss a "when" and demoralization followed.

What was always known at the beginning of these strategic planning meetings was the deadline or the "when" – 12 months. That was all the Man cared about. Gary knew though, that he had to incorporate mini "whens" through that year-long plan. A year was too long to wait to see if he won or lost or was even on the right path to their goals. His team had to have small wins and acknowledge any loss along the way. It kept the team's engine motivated and moving. "Whens" were so critical that he put most of his time strategizing on them. How did he do it? He took all the input, perspectives, and opinions from his team, combined those with what was going on in their business and marketplace and applied the worst-case scenario to it all. Plans and ambitions always start with optimism. While that is great and all, it is not realistic. Some red herring (fallacy) or black swan (unexpected development) or other waterfowl seems to try and knock the plan off its path. Considering and even anticipating those unpredictable and unforeseen events was the critical reality check necessary to determine the "when". Worst-case scenarios were the diamonds. It helped prep for the inevitable nasty unpredictables that aimed to destroy the "what", the "why", the "how" and the "when". Carefully calculating the timing of it all was the magic. Snap in a legitimate "when" while establishing a well devised and well-rounded "what", "why" and "how" plan was like finding gold.

Step Six: Where

This was the big logistics question. A lot of planners might say that determining the "where" – the place, the target, or the opportunity – should be first. Gary could understand that logic but liked to flip it upside down. He wanted 90 percent of his plan baked and then apply that plan to the "where" question last. If there were any major flaws or gaps or weaknesses in the previous 5 steps, the "where" would uncover them. This step was a bit more complicated because they had to apply all the steps above (What x 2, Why, How, When) to this one single subset. He would meld both approaches somewhere in the middle where they intersected. He could be sure that he came to a comprehensive plan by going at the revenue target from two very different places. It brought the plan full circle and once they were done, they were ready to get that 20 percent dollar growth target.

Leadership was a drive to making those intangibles a tangible objective that could be easily understood and clearly communicated with the rest of the organization. It didn't matter if the objective was fought over and debated by the strategic team. It only mattered that the fight culminated in agreement on a shared identity, being on the same page, and moving forward toward that singular point. Once the "what" (the point) was established, the "why's" (reason) communicated, the "how's" (mechanisms) collaboratively determined, the "when" snapped into place, and all applied to the "where" – that was planning. That was leadership!

The Pearl: The Six Step Plan – easy to use and easy to implement. Follow this plan in your personal and professional life and see a clear direction make its way for you.

16

TIME TO QUIT?

Gary fought hard for his concept of leadership. It was hard because the Man's way was so different and difficult. Why the hell would this be something that he would have to fight for? Nothing within his management approach was out of the ordinary. Countless books were written about what Gary was incorporating into his own approach. The easy answer was that the Man wasn't reading the same books and was not interested in the slightest to read or do anything new. The Man did not operate this way and was not about to change. He was not about anything other than being passive aggressive and running the salt mine like an Army General. Not to insult the demanding management style of an Army General, it has its place for sure, but in a simple sales organization, it didn't. The Man did not buy into or understand the concept of a "shared identity". What he was all in on was his identity and a "my way or the highway" style. Share MY identity or beat it!

Gary stayed late at night talking with the Man about the shared identity concept, its value, and its transformative ability to move to a goal quicker and more effortlessly. While the Man wanted to get there too (and make more money in doing so) he looked at Gary like he was speaking a foreign language. Gary felt forced to move his management style underground. Now this might seem like insubordination and mutiny. Many would say that Gary should have been fired. The Man is the Man and what the Man says goes. Period. To many, it did not matter how sincere Gary's intent was; he was hired by the Man and should fall in line right behind the Man's decisions or move on to another job. This might be true, but remember, Gary had not learned to quit yet, so he pressed on with his mutinous approach.

Gary's only intention was to deliver what the Man wanted but he knew that the only way to successfully do it was to get the organization to buy in to a plan to get there. If he got that buy-in from his team, he would limit dysfunction, build cohesive and unified harmony that would drive the team effortlessly to the objective. It was that simple. Getting everyone on the same page and for the same reasons using tactics they all agreed upon made the objective clear. It always had to be a team effort. While that is so obvious and so overused, Gary was faced with implementing that overused and commonsensical approach despite the Man's edict. It was going to take quite an effort to implement the plan without the Man's buy-in. The Man knew what he wanted. Nothing else mattered. Just get it done. No planning, no strategizing, no team-building necessary. Fuck all that. Just get to work and get it done. The edict!

What Gary should have done was quit and move on. He was never going to get the Man to be on the same page with where everyone else was. The Man was an immoveable object and quickly becoming the company's liability. What was he thinking? If the Man was not going to even try to understand what was needed to be done, why did he even bother? The Man had the last word. Without the Man's cooperation, Gary would have to operate two realities like a play on Broadway – one where the real effective hard work behind the curtain was taking place and everyone was working together in agreement on the corporate strategy and the other where a grand act on stage was showing the Man just what he wanted to see and hear. He was trying to both operate in the best interest of the Man and for the betterment of the company despite the Man. Most smart people would have understood this strategy was impossible to effectively perform and quit. Gary didn't. The impossible and untenable situation that resulted would create such dysfunction that it would paralyze the organization and put Gary in the hospital. The lesson from it all, though, would be invaluable to him for the rest of his career.

The Pearl: There is no clearer sign, pearl, or message, for you to move on than being in a dysfunctional environment or relationship. If you have attempted everything you can and there is still no change, there will never be a change. Recognize the sign and heed its message. Quit compromising and move on!

17

COMFORTABLY NUMB (FOOLING YOURSELF)

The truth was that Gary was comfortable. Even though he was working in a toxic and shitty environment, he was comfortable. He was making a great living, and he had a great group of people he had hired, trusted, and "mined" with. He was growing the business. His people were mostly happy, and the business was humming along progressively, although too slowly for his taste. He was so comfortable he was bored. The daily jousting sessions with the Man livened up his life a bit. He got energy from them – energy he was becoming subconsciously addicted to. It was energy that had no business in his life, but he couldn't do without. It was the juice to the boredom that masochistically made it all tolerable, at least temporarily.

Working everyday making love to comfort did not mean Gary was happy. He was far from that. Was it because of his situation, his job, the Man, or himself? Everything was on the table to consider, and Gary was willing to look into the mirror and accept his contribution to his own miserable comfort. Deep down, he knew it was him. It was his alpha personality type. The type of personality that was never satisfied, never content. While it served him with a drive that was incomparable, it made him restless. He would map out a goal, get it, and then start over again. He was a goal setter and a goal getter. But this was becoming an endless cycle and he felt that once the small celebration ended after getting to a goal, he really was left empty. Achieving the goal felt good, but once he got to it, he felt the pressure to outdo it. The achieved goal would become ground zero and he would plug away again.

Gary often imagined himself as someone else – someone who was happy with what he had. He wanted to be someone who got to a goal and was satisfied and didn't try to push on and do it again faster and better. Life must be so much easier for those people. They achieved some sort of success that was satisfying to them, and they simply stayed there, happy, content, and comfortable. While Gary envied that, it made him anxious to think of himself in that reality. That would be so foreign. He was comfortable in the maniacal cycle that was silently killing him. Contentment seemed boring based on his energy addiction. But he wanted the peace that he envisioned came with contentment. The energy had to go. It was what had fueled him, but it was always what was leaving him empty and on the never-ending ride. He needed to get the energy needle out of his vein. He needed to break the addiction. It kind of scared him. If it was scary, it was probably worth doing, he thought. Being content. An interesting dream. A new goal!

Professional comfort was a tricky thing. It seemed that comfort was what everyone always aspired to have. To be professionally comfortable meant achievement of some level of success, status, or position. Gary built an operation and a business that just hummed successfully along. He drove a nice car, lived in a nice house, had a dog, went out to eat whenever he wanted and even considered flying first class. Money wasn't a worry. Money was there when needed and because of its existence it gave him the right to choose. He didn't have to stress or compromise anymore because the money in his pocket allowed him the freedom to now choose and rarely deal with an uncomfortable choice. To be financially comfortable meant he had "made" it. Gary the envy of family, friends, neighbors, and strangers, living the dream. But comfort, Gary was quickly learning, was a conniving, persuasive, sly, hypnotic, crafty, and seductive predator. It was kind of like Kaa, the coy character in the Disney cartoon version of The Jungle Book. Kaa, the snake, tried to trap Mowgli in his coils by hypnotizing him with his eyes and singing, "Trust in Me." He wanted to lull the little man-cub to sleep so he could eat him. Comfort, to Gary, was beginning to look, feel and sound a lot like Kaa.

Gary seemed to be sliding into a trance himself and the false happiness that feeling this comfort maternally provided. He was gently gliding down to apathy's abyss and before he knew it, he was drowning in every comfort synonym – indifference, lethargy, laziness, boredom, stagnancy and, yes, ennui: a feeling of weariness and dissatisfaction. It was who he had become, the Ennui Man, the superhero! He fought the uninspired trance. He painted on a smile and acted out the energetic ambition his people deserved but deep down, his comfort was uninspiring like a rock dropped into a river. It fell right to the bottom and was covered in silt while the water, and life itself, rushed on without him. How could this be? He worked so hard to get to that "comfort". Shouldn't he be satisfied? He worked so hard to get to such a successful career peak and found he wasn't living at all. He was just processing air.

To get to that successful professional point in his life was a battle. It was hard! He felt like he had been beaten, battered, and bruised along the way to get to comfort, and while he would quickly admit he was better for it and even proud of it, he felt unfulfilled, unsuccessful, and apathetic. But wasn't Gary following the well-used, well-travelled blueprint to success that others traversed and were respected and admired for? What the fuck? Life was hard, get used to it. He heard that from everywhere. "If it ain't hard, you ain't doing something right." That was the message that was always taught and what everyone understood as true. So, Gary went through professional hell, achieved status, respect, riches and ultimately disappointment. Disappointment! What the fuck? The "life was hard," mantra pulsed through everyone's veins and seeped right through everyone's pores. That mantra, coupled with the "don't quit" messages pounded in Gary's head from everywhere. The "life was hard" combo was a one-two sucker punch to the groin. Taking the hard road was admired and revered, and something to be proud of and respected for. How many people have talked about their meager and humble beginnings and what monumental feats it took to get to where they were? Everyone admired a hard-knock story. Rags to riches baby! Remember Rocky? There were eight movies in that film series that knocked viewers out with the tag team duo of, "don't quit" and "life was hard." It was inspiring and it has become a part of our culture.

Of course, it is inspiring to hear a story about how someone overcame massive obstacles and terrible hardships to achieve greatness. Gary was fueled on by these incredible stories. What Gary was beginning to discover though, was that it didn't have to be this way.

> "Nothing in the world is worth having or worth doing unless it means effort, pain, difficulty...I have never in my life envied a human being who led an easy life. I have envied a great many people who led difficult lives and led them well."
>
> — T. ROOSEVELT

How the hell can one of the most iconic United States presidents in American history be argued with? Those 46 words summed it all up.

And what about this little peach of a lyric from Steve Miller's "Jet Airliner":

> But my heart keeps calling me backwards,
> As I get on the 707,
> Ridin' high I got tears in my eyes,
> You know you got to go through hell,
> Before you get to heaven.

People lived their lives by it. Gary was no longer buying it though. He just did it and felt like poop. He went down the hard road, dealt with crappy situations and tough issues, achieved unimaginable success and it just didn't matter. The road that got him to where he got to was rife with potholes and monsters and pointed straight up hill. He was supposed to feel a great sense of accomplishment for getting through such a road; that is what the quote and everyone else said would happen. He just felt nothing.

He was not going to go as far as taking advice from another great American icon, Homer Simpson, who once said, "If something's hard to do, then it's not worth doing." That was not the point at all. The epiphany that Gary was coming to was that just because it was easy, did not mean you shouldn't do it.

Taking the hard road was not always advisable even though it may have been the most admired. Fuck that! It might be easy because of a situation Gary may have simply put himself in. It may be easy because his skills and strengths gave him the ability to create an easy road. Maybe he was just a natural. There is nothing wrong with that. Judge all you want! No one should ever be judged for that. Often, when people made things look easy, it was due to a lot of focused effort, simple luck, and God-given talent. It didn't have to be hard to be worthwhile. It doesn't have to be hard to feel a sense of accomplishment. And if it is too hard, he could quit, and not feel judged as a loser. Gary was beginning to feel that as long as the "hard" was not attributed to being lazy or becoming a self-saboteur, then quitting and moving on was undeniably becoming an option.

Gary's epiphany involved the realization that a majority of his "hard" was a matter of three very absent elements in his own life. Three elements that were rarely a product of a situation, a circumstance, other people, or an environment he was immersed in. This bummed his "blame it on another" tendencies. For example, a "hard" could be as simple as the weather: "I am so miserable. Three days of grey skies and bone splitting cold." Alternatively, the blame could be directed at a supervisor: "I hate my job. It is so hard to deal with my boss. He is a relentless bully and thankless MOFO." Or the blame could be placed on fate: "I cannot believe the cards I have been dealt. This is just terrible. Why does everything have to be so hard? Life sucks!" Just three examples floating around in a sea of a million examples of "hard." They all had one common trait he realized – that guy in the mirror, the self-saboteur. It's a great name for a rock band but not a great characteristic to embrace, cultivate and live by. He was doing all of those in a beautifully demonstrated daily tango. The self-saboteur that was a master Jedi at dismissing those three elements daily and as a result experiencing the wonders of "hard" regularly.

In no particular order, those three elements were perspective, trust, and belief. Without those three elements, "hard" was everywhere.

Perspective: When Gary forced himself to change his perspective from a negative outlook and outcome to positive ones, he realized something incredible. This was not an easy adjustment by the way. This was not natural or in his nature. He generally approached challenges from a worst-case scenario point of view. Expecting the worst and getting a positive outcome was always serendipity. He lived for serendipity. But that was not a way to live life and approach tough situations. It destroyed the present while he worried about the future. While considering the worst-case scenario in every decision-making process had value and gave him a holistic perspective on a situation, only considering a worst-case scenario was debilitating, short sighted and unfair. He was fooling himself. It made the tough situation tougher and the present unbearable to live through. He tended to approach challenges from a worst-case scenario, especially if they were hard. But when he changed his perspective on "hard" from a "challenge" to an "opportunity," one thing happened almost immediately: the result always had a positive personal impact. Always. If he won, that positive perspective gave him the best odds to win. If he lost and maintained that positive perspective, he always found the pearl of good out of the bad. He knew to look for it and the value the loss brought to future wins. This was perspective. Bring a positive perspective to any situation and Gary gave himself the best opportunity to get a positive outcome regardless of the result. His positive perspective would turn any negative result into a learning opportunity, and he changed his approach and his outcome. Bring a negative perspective to anything, and "hard" will get harder because thoughts become things.

Trust: This meant letting go of trying to control what he could not control or worry about what he could not affect. He just had to have confidence that the universe had got his back regardless of the outcome. Whatever the outcome, have the trust to accept the outcome and not label it good or bad. It just was. He just had to do his best and have trust that the outcome was what it was and that the result has value for his life. Accept it. It felt refreshing. He didn't have to control everything if he just had trust that whatever happened, happened for a reason even if he did not understand or know the reason at the time.

Belief. This was the toughest one. This one differed from trust in that it was personal. Trust was about letting go of things that he could not control and just let them unfold and accept the result as it was. He learned to stop trying to control the uncontrollable. Belief had to do with his soul. He had direct influence there. He could control that. He embraced the belief in himself that he COULD. He made it undeniable and made it happen. He could not be beat when he believed in himself. This required a major rewiring or rerouting of Gary's life path and mindset. He had created deep behavioral ruts in his life's path that would take a lot of time and self-convincing to fill in and redo. He was ready for a big step though. If he took tiny steps to move closer to believing in himself, he would be dead by the time he got there. This step involved a full jump into unadulterated belief. Why not? It would only serve him well, so why was it so fucking hard to change his path? Gary committed himself to the big step just like he had committed to jumping out of the plane. The next step was really going to be easy, but he would have to employ an exercise to develop this new thought behavior. Like developing any new routine, this would require consistent and pig-headed dedication. He was up for it. If someone wants to build muscle, they must work out regularly. Muscles were not going to grow and change by themselves. If he was going to change this tendency, he was going to have to work out his soul regularly. He knew that he just couldn't take a pill and get instant belief, although that sounded awesome. He committed to the one thing that came to mind to fill in these ruts – talking to himself. That was going to be the exercise he was going to undertake. Like repeating bicep curls to build his arms, he was going to work on his mind over and over again. Repeat it until he believed it, and then attract it.

Yes, he was going to talk to himself out loud and every chance he got. He did not care if people around him would think he was nuts. He could see people just stepping aside as he talked to himself. It might just serendipitously put him to the front of a long line he was waiting in. He knew he would get stared at and hear murmurs such as, "I think that guy is nuts! He keeps talking to himself telling himself how wonderful he is and that his future is bright." But talking to himself was going to be the exercise he was going to do until he carved a new, more positive path in his life.

His verbal exercise reps sounded a bit like this:

> *"I'm good. The universe has got my back. Everything is going to be groovy. I am a good guy, and I can do anything in the face of any adversity. I am thankful for all that I have."*

He was going to repeat this or something like this every chance he got until he was convinced of the words he heard coming out of his mouth. Once was never going to be enough. Just like one bicep curl would not give him head-turning guns, saying this just once was not going to move the needle anywhere.

All of this made Gary feel like he was fooling himself by diving into unharnessed optimism, accepting results as they were and just flat out believing in himself. The self-saboteur was lurking right over his shoulder incessantly whispering quietly, "C'mon Gary. Just keep approaching people and things with the worst-case scenario. All bad ahead. C'mon Gary, you are all you got. There is no universe. You can control everything. No one has your back. You got you. That's it. Universe? What is that? C'mon Gary, believe in yourself? Whatever. Disbelieve in yourself. You aren't capable. You are too (fill in the blank with a negative here): _____. It's not about CAN but it is always about CAN'T." He had been living with this self-saboteur his whole life. Kicking it out of his life was going to require a major jump and a lot of talking to himself. Next time he would get a visit from this self-inflicted personal demon, he promised himself to acknowledge his entry and then bid him goodbye. It would take a lot of goodbyes and he knew it. He was done with fooling himself in the negative. If he was going to fool himself any longer, it would be with light-hearted optimism. He had to be for himself. No one else was going to do it for him.

A comfortable summit. It was confounding. He really wasn't experiencing the positive side of comfort: ease, peace, well-being, relief. Why? What he didn't know was that comfort was masquerading as a peak, but he was just on a professional plateau. He was nowhere near the peak or summit of anything. It took Gary to quit and move on to finally understand the witchy nature of comfort and the value discomfort brought once he decided to accept and embrace it.

The Pearl: Fool yourself in the positive. It is all about Perspective, Trust, and Belief.

18

DYSFUNCTION

Working at the salt mine brought a lot of value to Gary's personal and professional life. Some of that value was expected. He learned to manage people and build a business. He learned how to outmaneuver his competition. He made money. He learned how to lead. But there were other, not so anticipated nuggets of value, that while he dealt with them basically sucked ass, but as he worked through them, he acquired skills that he could never imagine.

Narcissism, lack of leadership, megalomania, and greed. Being a student of those behaviors reaped great lessons on how not to operate or behave. Another wonderful, blind-sided subject he got a front-row seat to learn from and deal with was passive aggressiveness. An oxymoronic behavior that made his head spin. Make no mistake, someone who is passive aggressive was doing him deliberately behind a grin. Add a healthy, heaping dash of narcissism and Gary had a full-blown cancer planted right on his groin. Anyone have any salve for Christ's sake? Unfortunately, salve wouldn't help him. Superman couldn't help him either. He had to use his wits, patience, and a herculean perseverance to win that battle or just quit being around that kind of person and save himself the effort. Gary, at the time didn't know how to do that obviously.

The Man was a passive aggressive predator. The truth was that his resentment grew with each dollar that Gary put in his pocket. As the company began to grow, the success could be directly attributed to Gary's willingness to be open to change, create a collaborative environment and to keep pace with the ever-changing business market they were making a living in. The Man resented Gary for essentially becoming the leader he was not and understanding the business in a way that he didn't. The always say "no" first and "my way or the highway" days were fading and a culture of "yes" and "we aren't the best because we can always be better" was taking hold of everyone.

If the Man was anything, he was king of the jungle at the art of smiling angrily behind the rim of a paper coffee cup. As he listened, he would raise a cup to his mouth and chew on the rim. His eyes would peer over the cup as he fed on the speaker with his gaze. The glare over the coffee cup was like the look of a lion in the Serengeti peering at its prey through the bush in the middle of the night at an oblivious future meal. The look was thoughtful. He was intently listening. But behind the pensive look, the thoughts were filled with resentment, anger, and pressure. It was scary! It was subtle and toxic. The surface look made Gary feel like he was being heard and validated. But when Gary would leave the meeting, the Man would put his gnarled cup down and make decisions and give directions completely counter to what he had just discussed and agreed to with Gary.

The Man was angry at his self-described protégé. The protégé was causing him to lose his relevancy at the salt mine. That would have sucked for anyone – losing their perceived importance, especially with their own business, is a blow to the ego and to the soul. How one deals with this though is their true character. Gary could tell the character of people by the way they handle the bad. How someone handled the good never showed you much. When everything is hunky-dory, isn't everyone happy and on their best behavior? It is when the shit hits the fan or when something bad happens that Gary got a clear picture inside someone. What was happening at the salt mine was good, but the Man was not at the center of all the good things happening. He felt irrelevant. So, he would bully his way into a conversation or create drama to make sure everyone still knew he was there. The salt mine just put up with him and couldn't wait for him to take a day off. All Gary was doing was building a business. He was getting exposed to anything and everything to get better. He was making the Man rich. The Man was busy sitting in his office scheming how he was going to try and keep the money flowing in while regaining his importance in the business. All the Man really had to do was to get humble. Instead, he became more egotistical and insolent. A "grateful" approach to one's perceived irrelevance can bring tremendous understanding because of that display of vulnerability. Hey, so the Man didn't know all the answers and he wasn't at the center of the universe. All he had to do was to admit that was how he felt. His team would rally and embrace him and get him back into relevance in no time. His team always had his back if he showed that he trusted them enough to share those insecurities and vulnerabilities. Narcissists don't suffer these fools. The Man remained irrelevant.

Gary was doing the same thing to the Man as well. He would give nods of understanding and approval at the Man's instructions. Then, when he left the meeting, he forgot all of it and continued with his own strategic plan. It made for a very toxic situation and relationship. Gary knew he was contributing to it and had a part in all the dysfunction. It was why he should have quit sooner. Being put into that type of situation, or worse still putting himself in such a circumstance, should have told him that it was TIME TO GO!

> **The Pearl**: You can be bitter from the experience of bad events and situations that happen in your life. You can harbor a lot of resentment for what you had to go through because of them. It is hard not to, but what good does it really do you? Recognize the 'pearls' that come out of the bad. They are always there as long as you make yourself aware of them. Those pearls make you better, stronger, and wiser. One way to **win big** is to recognize the lessons (pearls) from the bad while they are happening. By being aware of the good while going through the bad, you will dampen the difficult situation

and it will help you get through your circumstances faster.

SWEET SUGAR

Sugar! Who can resist it? Most of us could call sugar one of our very own personal indulgent vices. We eat it for fun. We eat it when we are stressed. We eat it when we are bored. We eat it when we are sad, and we eat it when we are mad. We eat it just because we can. It is easy, tastes great, comes in a million different magnificent forms, and can be devoured at any time of the day. It makes us happy. Well, maybe for just a little bit but that little bit is so awesome.

We never eat it when we are trying to get better though, do we? If we want to lose weight, there are no diets out there that include sugar. When we want to get stronger, cleaner, and live a healthier lifestyle, sugar has little to do with any of those endeavors. You can see a body built on sugar from a mile away.

Diets made of sugar, after the initial endorphin rush, make people sluggish, susceptible to weight gain, give them rotten teeth, diabetes, and lead to a whole host of other undesirable consequences. Life ain't fair! Why can't sugar be good for you? But a diet without sugar, simply makes you feel stronger, better, smarter, more alert, faster, leaner, meaner, and so on. Have you ever seen an Olympian refer to sugar being a key ingredient to their gold medal victory? Exactly!

Businesses are also susceptible to the sugar high of an easy buck and if they are not careful, they can get fat, gluttonous, complacent, lazy, and out of business. Organizations built on immediate gratification of the sugar are built upon a foundation of sugary pixie sticks – that candy you pour into your mouth from a straw shaped wrapper. Yummy! All that goodness wrapped in dextrose, citric acid, and artificial and natural flavors. It builds the body good for sure. Ever see a business built on this type of instant gratification weather a change in the market, a new competitor, or a sales slump? They don't. They are only as good as their last transaction.

The Man's business was a business built on this exact foundation. It was cheap to build and easy to run. It operated on the backs and the sweat of cheap, commission-only labor, which required little investment and a whole lot of swagger. The over used analogy of the sinking Titanic is appropriate here. The Man's company was heading for an iceberg but unlike the Titanic story, everyone saw it, except the Man. The Titanic was built of steel. Steel would cost too much for the Man's ship. His vessel was built on ego and his arrogance was the iceberg.

If the only value a business offered was that it had the lowest price in the market, the business was built on sugar. If the only value an organization possessed was maintaining the lowest price in the market, the business was built on sugar. While maintaining the lowest price, revenues skyrocketed. Everyone bought from the low-price leader, right? Sugar in the business was just a price. No value. It lasted as long as the transaction and then evaporated after the sale was done. The transaction was valuable to the customer only because the business just happened to have the lowest price at the moment of purchase. Substance was equated to a value the customer just could not do without. But what happened when that was the only value and when a dirty, good for nothing, mouth breathing, competitor decided to challenge the company's lowest price with a lower price of their own? Catastrophe. Without taking the quick sugar rush revenue gains resulting from having the lowest price and metabolizing them into value, substance, or meat, the company's days were numbered. It was just a matter of time. What happens next? The valueless business doubles down on sale price. The office is furnished with third-hand furniture, the heat is turned down, the "think" signs go up on the wall, and any other empty wall space is littered with "never, ever, ever quit" inspirational messages. It is impossible to continue to turn out the volume of transactions needed to keep the ship built on ego afloat. This was what was happening to the Man's business.

He didn't invest in substance to provide more diversified value to customers or invest in his people to make them feel valued. They were mules hauling sugar. The Man's value was built on price and once that price was beaten by someone else, those customers quickly went to that someone else. Because most of what Gary did was to educate himself about competitors, trends, and the marketplace, he knew that the Man's strategy was going to sink them all. It was only a matter of time; those sugar infused revenues were going to get a bad case of diabetes.

How does someone become a lean, mean fighting machine? Well, eating right. Eating right involves preparing and devouring nutrients of substance. We are talking about vegetables, lean protein, few carbohydrates and little, if any, sugar. How does a business become a lean, mean fighting company? By building the business on value-principles. Profits from the sugar should be reinvested into value services to get away from being a low-priced leader of anything. Charging big rates coupled with personal service and the value offered in exchange will make customers feel better for having engaged with your organization. Because the Man was only in business to line his own pockets and to donate his sugar to his favorite special interests that would be blind to his narcissism, the business was passed by the times, developments in the market, competition, and customers.

Gary was not allowed to leverage the company's sugar success and double down on real customer value to grow faster and with more substance. This was the way any successful entrepreneur built the real meat and potatoes of the business. The Man controlled the speed and cared little for substance. To provide value meant investing in skills, human capital, and offers that had little to do with price and more to do with service and value that benefited the customer. The company narcissist didn't give two shits about what benefitted anyone but himself. Substance cost money. Sugar was easier to attain. Sugar only cost blood, sweat and a few tears from his salespeople. Sugar could be put on the company marquee and be bragged about. "Look at those great revenue numbers we have," the Man would expound to everyone. Gary knew that living on a sugar revenue diet was not sustainable. He was living and telling lies about how incredible the company was based on this sugar. Bragging about revenues founded on a pile of sugar, and not supported by real value and substance, was like living in a house made of pixie sticks.

The Man thought he was moving fast, but that just showed how out of touch he really was. Part of the reason for that out-of-touch circumstance had to do with the fact that the Man never went out anywhere. He was the master within the walls of the salt mine. There was nothing out there in the industry that could teach him anything. The Man knew everything and if something were developing out there in the marketplace, it would come to him. What the Man didn't know was that neither he nor the business was the best outside of those salt mine walls. That scared the shit out of Gary. He was not heard when he talked about the business threats that were lurking in plain sight or the opportunities he had positioned the company to take advantage of. He would often go home and think to himself, "How can I do 'enough' if I am never heard? I am not doing what's necessary. I am not doing enough!" He was sounding like the annoying "never do enough" voice of the Man. What a role reversal! He already put the pressure on himself to do more. He didn't need the Man to do that for him. It really showed him how much the Man didn't know him at all, because if he had, he would not have subjected him to the constant scrutiny and late Friday afternoon ball busting sessions.

To a large degree, Gary leveraged the Man's drive to counterbalance his own growth and mind-numbing disillusionment. He was oddly thankful for the Man's tireless sugar ambition and consumption. It knocked some of the apathetic rust collecting on his conscience. Gary was thankful but not inspired. This wasn't an inspirational ambition the Man exuded. His was a take no prisoners, F your mother type of ambition. Gary was allergic to that. It drove a wall between him and the Man. So, while on the one hand, it helped push him, on the other it just made him disillusioned and feel gross. Why hadn't he quit? What was the problem? It was clear to everyone around him. His situation was just untenable. Was it the comfort? Maybe. He could not deny his standard of living brought him things and an ego boost. Or was it failure? Bingo! Gary knew that the situation was tough and if he did not overcome the challenge, it meant he failed. He had to pivot the company from the addiction to sugar. How delusional was that? He only realized the extent of the delusion the day after he finally moved on.

Just move on. Those were the three words that changed his outlook on quitting. While those three words could absolutely be defined as "quit", they had an optimistic sound to them that Gary liked. It meant a look to the future instead of regretting a past. It meant cutting the cord of the past, moving on and tethering to hope. The seed was planted, and he began to attract a strategy that would allow him to finally move on.

What was ironic about the salt mine, or rather, sugar mine was that the Man had a pet name for his wife. It just so happened to be, "Sugar." He would introduce her to everyone that way – a new member at the club, the priest at his church, and new employees. She even got so wrapped up in the pet name that she introduced herself as Sugar, shedding the name she had before she married the Man. You were to call her Sugar when you saw her. Narcissism ran deep and sweet in Sugar.

The Pearl: Sugar. While it is so good, it is so bad for you personally and professionally. Are you living in a sugar mine? Get aware of it, then begin to think of the small steps you can take to move on. If you stay, your condition will never improve.

20

THE MOVE AND THE PLAN

Before moving on from his job entirely, he thought he would first begin to list all the things he was doing to contribute to his misery in the first place. It wasn't just one thing. It wasn't just the Man. So, he would identify them, perform an introspective search and hone in on all the things he had to move on from in order to find happiness. Maybe, if he was able to identity all the little pieces- all the ingredients to the complete misery pie – and move on from them, he might find that his overall job was just fine and that the Man wasn't the lynchpin to it all.

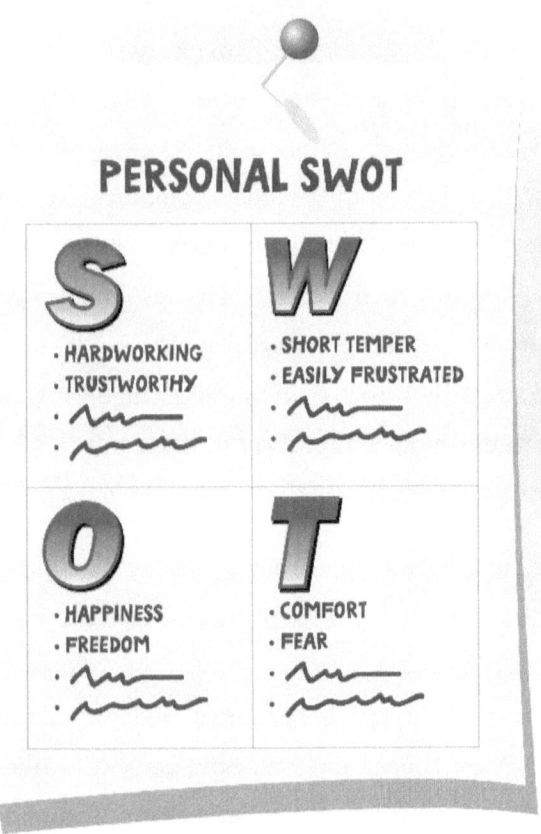

Step 1: If he was going to quit something, or move on from something, he had to replace it with something else. That was going to be the first thing he was going to do. This was going to be tough. This action entailed looking truly at himself and changing habits. Habits were big things. They were rooted in routine, and they were built upon a sturdy foundation of

comfort. Comfort was #1 on Gary's Most Wanted Quit list. He wasn't going to be able to capture that #1 until he worked his way through the process of looking at everything he was doing. Pretty difficult to step outside of himself, observe and then change. He was going to do his own personal SWOT analysis, that Strength, Weakness, Opportunity, and Threat strategic introspection that many companies use to strategically grow their business. He was going to strategically grow himself and move toward happiness. This was the only way he knew how to step forward strange as it might have seemed to incorporate a standard business practice for personal growth.

He took out a piece of paper, drew a vertical line and intersected it with a horizontal one creating four quadrants. He wrote Strength, Weakness, Opportunity, and Threat in each respective quadrant and then stopped. He knew that some of his strengths were tapped out and now actually weaknesses. His weaknesses were those very intimate characteristics he hated to admit to but knew that he had to work on and address head on. He was going to have to marinate in honestly thinking about his strengths and weaknesses. So, he skipped those for the time being and went straight to the "O" and "T" parts of the quadrant.

Opportunity would be easy. He had already identified that, and those items were the reason why he was going through this personal SWOT analysis in the first place. He listed them out: freedom, doing something that matters, making a difference and happiness. Those were the opportunities that were driving him to move on. He was inspired just thinking about them.

Threat was also an easy one. He knew if he faced the threats head on, and if he had the courage, that his opportunities would unfold effortlessly before him. He wrote fear and comfort. These two words were the threats keeping him wedged down into one place unable to move. Comfort lulled him to sleep while fear stopped him from even thinking about getting out of the wedge.

Back to the "S" and "W." Strengths and weaknesses were going to be tough to self-determine. He basically knew them but either had a hard time admitting to them or felt he could not be completely honest with himself identifying them. So, he decided he would make his peers, friends and family do them for him. He knew that he could not be completely honest with himself even as hard as he might try to fill in these two quadrants. He knew he would either water down his weaknesses or omit them altogether. He would amplify his strengths and probably just get carried away. This had to be a pure and honest exercise and he knew, as open as he was to change, that he ran the risk of not completely being truthful with himself in his own description of his strengths and weaknesses. He feared what his peers, friends and family would say but if he was going to change, he had to know everything.

How could he change something if he didn't even know he was doing something wrong? He had to ask the people around him for that outside personal critique. So, Gary went to his family, his friends and his colleagues and asked them, "Could you write down my strengths and weaknesses?" Gary's toes curled each time he asked, and he smiled in embarrassed fright awaiting their responses. He knew that all parties involved would benefit from this exercise. If he didn't take offense to the weaknesses, his opportunity to grow and improve would be mind-blowing. He knew that as far as strengths and weaknesses went, depending on the situation, his weaknesses were sometimes his strengths, and his strengths were sometimes his weaknesses. All those traits created who he was and who the people closest to him loved.

What he got back was:

Strengths: Hardworking, trustworthy, dedicated, strong-willed, loving, smart, driven, loyal, and curious. They also stated that he gave a 100% to whatever he did, was a leader, eloquent, self-motivated, considerate, and responsible.

Weaknesses: short tempered, easily frustrated, sometimes doesn't pay attention when talked to, won't admit when wrong, impatient, easily triggered, overly sensitive, takes things too personally, and doesn't take comments or criticism easily.

So, there it was. He got what he asked for and it stung a little, but he knew it was a step to understand what he had to work on and what he had to move away from to move forward. Some of the weaknesses that were listed for him surprised him. He was doing some things and acting in some ways that were negatively affecting the people around him and he didn't even know it. Now he knew. Now he could take action.

Step 2, in no particular order, he was going to look at his life. He would look at his personal relationships and habits and his professional ones too. He would analyze the "hows" of "what" he was doing and the "whys" of those "hows". He would catch his thoughts because he knew thoughts became things. He had always read that when someone changed their beliefs, they changed their life. Change your attitude and things before you transform themselves to something interesting.

Following the example from his covert strategic planning method at the salt mine, he answered the What, Why, How, When and Where questions as they pertained to his personal plan.

> **What (do I want) (Part I):** Freedom and to make a difference. The product of those two would be happiness.
> **What (I don't want) (Part II):** He didn't want to be around anyone that looked and acted like the Man. Goodbye to toxic narcissists. He didn't want to be held back by fear and comfort anymore.
> **Why:** Because it was time to live and connect with others and shed fear and comfort from stopping him from reaching his dreams. Living from his heart gave

him the fulfillment he was seeking from his life. Living from his heart was the best version of himself.

How: Perform a personal SWOT. Fool himself in the positive. Change his perspective to the positive with everything he encountered. Have trust in the universe to handle all the things he had no control over. Believe in himself and talk to himself until he was convinced of it. Challenge comfort's embrace and forget about fear. Move on from his job.

When: One month. It was ambitious but it was too late for small steps. What was there really to worry about if he changed his perspective, had trust, and believed in himself? Just like the first words in this book, it was time for big leaps! Fuck it. He was going for it.

Where: Right here, right now!

The Pearl: The Equation: The personal SWOT + Quit a bad habit and replace + the 6-question plan = freedom with a dash of uncomfortable + happiness.

21

TIME TO STOP

Writing down his habits was more challenging than Gary thought. He wanted to be honest with himself and identify all the habits that made up his actions whether they were positive or negative. He was going to look at what he did personally and professionally. For his positive habits, he thought he would list them and just be thankful for them. For all he knew, they were positive, although someone else might tell him otherwise. He had to go with his gut on what he felt served him and everyone around him. He would not take them for granted. Whether it was exercising, eating healthy, not smoking, treating people with kindness, being considerate, committing to a decision and so on, he was a little humbled by admitting these to himself and he was thankful.

For the not so positive habits he was going to identify them, take action and replace them; this proposal seemed unusually easy. The fact that it was easy was disappointing because this meant that he was aware of his bad habits that were not serving him or anyone one around him, but he continued to perpetuate them. Okay, time to stop that. On the surface, many of his habits seemed harmless, but they were harming him. So, he started his list.

He brainstormed:

Offering Advice. He would stop doing it except in cases where he was clearly asked. Not that giving advice was necessarily a bad thing, but it was not always the right thing and quite frankly opinions were like assholes – everyone has them. He had learned about giving advice from the Man. The Man was a self-promoted problem solver, one of the best. It didn't matter what he talked about, he was going to give advice whether anyone wanted it or not. Even when Gary was just trying to shoot the shit with him, he would try to solve the problem within the conversation. Most of the time Gary just wanted to talk and be heard. Sometimes, someone just wants to be heard and get it off their chest. Being there for someone without comment, opinion or solution could be even more appreciated and valuable. So, he was quitting the unadulterated habit of offering advice and replacing it with listening. Seemed easy enough, right?

Hustle: If anyone wanted a thriving business they had to hustle. It was the key ingredient in the development and operation of the machine. Hustlers act. Hustlers take immediate initiative.

Hustlers think – they are always thinking, strategizing, plotting. They don't need a sign on every wall telling them to THINK! Hustlers never try, they just do. Hustlers maneuver up and around and over a challenge. And, by the way, a challenge is always an opportunity to a hustler. They are never defined by a job description. They are the job description. No one gets a Hustle degree at a 4-year university, although being a hustler can get you any degree you want at any university. Hustle is the very sexy word that makes the world go around. The best hustlers move mountains where others cannot. Hustlers have style and swagger and operate with a humble confidence that leads from their hearts. They can't be beaten by anyone other than themselves.

Why would hustling be a habit to replace? Seemed like it did amazing things. Well, you would have a point, but hustling can be that habit that keeps you in a frenzy forgetting the moment and ignoring the person talking right in front of you. Hustlers are always looking forward to ruining the present with expectations of the future. They try to be all things to all people all the time, and while they have success at keeping the hundred balls in the air at the same time, they drop all the important ones. The energy addiction that hustle generates is probably akin to a constant shot of cocaine. Now that can't be healthy! It is self-powered, self-directed, self-absorbed, and self-destructive. That is how the hustler gets beat.

In business, while hustle can get the operation off the launching pad and in and out of trouble effortlessly, it, unfortunately, is not scalable. If your business or you are over-committed to the hustle, the grave awaits. Hustlers burn bright, they burn hot and then they burn out. If they are not careful to recognize the apex of their "self" efforts, the downward turn is more like a nosedive than a gentle glide in for landing. Unfortunately, a lot of people don't realize that their hustle can be their worst enemy at some point in their career. They point to hustle as being their best trait, their best habit. Like "comfort," "hustle" was a dangerous mistress.

Hustling was becoming a big problem for Gary. He had literally hustled it all at the salt mine. He started from the bottom and as he rose to the top, he took all the things that he did with him on the way. He was an Olympic 100-meter sprinter, always. He was buried going from one duty to the next and on his way to the next, he missed fat opportunities that were right in front of him. When he wasn't at the salt mine, his mind was on the salt mine and what had to be hustled the next day and what wasn't hustled the day before. Do you think Gary slept? You don't sleep when you are a hustler. Gary's mind didn't live in the present unless that present was so engaging that he could keep reins on his racing mind. Sleep required being in the moment. Gary was an insomniac.

As a hustler Gary had to control everything, trust few and do everything himself if it was going to get done quickly and correctly. He knew how to do tasks best. He got juiced trying to do a dozen things at once and having them all completed at the same time.

It was time to let go of this habit. Find more moderation. Find more time for the present. Give his heart and mind a break. Give all the people around him a break too. There had to be a

12-step process for getting off the hustle addiction. He felt like he could take the first step on getting off this track and to do it was by delegating. It may have been a small step, but it was a step, and that was all that counted in quitting this habit.

Delegating: Duh! What a revelation right? But delegating had a ton of traps that could turn the delegator back into a hustler really quickly.

If you have done any delegating yourself, you get the drill. You, the "delegator'" take the time out to meticulously train someone to do a task. That someone is the "delegate." The "delegatee" then proceeds to do the task while you, the "delegator," could shift your focus and attention to more pressing things and forget about the newly assigned duty. Yahoo! You were free. Wrong! You knew in the back of your mind that the "delegatee" would screw up and do it incorrectly, without attention to detail. It all just cost you more time and energy to redo, regroup and untangle what the "delegatee" did. On top of that unnerving development, all the time you took to train said "delegatee" was now completely wasted and you beat yourself up for even thinking about delegating in the first place. You could have basically done it yourself perfectly and moved on to the next item on your hustle list. You would then quietly blame the "delegatee" and then hustle and do the task yourself. Delegating, like this, was "hustle" in disguise. This didn't work.

There was to be a better way, for sure, and thousands of executives delegated with no problems. Gary was creating this problem. This had nothing to do with anything other than his own feeling of control and anxiety to hustle through all the tasks that had to be done in that second. The business needed more strategic attention and his personal life was taking a dive because he was just emotionally hustle-exhausted.

While Gary intended to replace "hustle" with "delegating" he knew that before he could really do it effectively, and avoid the "drill," he had to add one more element to do it right. This was probably obvious to all, but without first "inspecting," delegating was just hustle. He would let the work get done but swoop in at a milestone, inspect, correct if needed, and move on. While this would not lighten his workload initially, this would give him the freedom from doing all the work himself and the "delegate" would learn by doing. Gary planned to regularly intervene to catch any issue as it happened. He could use that mini-step approach to train on the way. Inspecting at each step assured he wouldn't be surprised by any outcome because he could steer the activity to the desired result. Now he could focus on the big picture. Delegating would allow him to get off the hustle-train and more effectively shift focus on what mattered. It would also empower the "delegatee" who would feel valued, trusted, and ultimately important to the team.

Being shy is a challenge in business. Gary, although he led a nice sized sales organization and gave many presentations and sales pitches daily, was painfully shy. His shyness was often perceived as being aloof and arrogant. He was neither and hated to be judged that way, but he knew he was creating that misperception himself. He was going to quit self-sabotaging himself, take a huge uncomfortable and awkward step from being shy, and replace it with a game that would help him overcome this bad habit. He would make a person a day, whether they were strangers or not, smile back at him. He would initiate the contact, something shy people are allergic to, and smile at them first. If he practiced this daily, he would get comfortable and greet everyone he passed with a smile. That smile would probably lead to some other interaction that would be the starting blocks of a relationship. The shyness would subside and the gifts that came from being open to others would flood in. The gifts from this simple and positive action and the continual practice of it would eventually become just an ordinary thing. Gary would, at all times and in all places, be the first to smile.

Complaining: This is ever-present in business but is never productive. Gary was going to stop it. Gary had worked so long in the salt mine, or sugar mine, that he no longer knew if he was working in a good or bad environment. It was all the same to him. He was a product of and contributor to the bad as much as he was a contributor to the good. Instead of Gary recognizing that he was surrounded by bad and running away from it, he just decided to complain about it, further contributing to the toxic environment. Complaining came out of feeling sorry for himself, not being happy, playing the part of the victim and perceiving "hard." Gary was the poster child of complaining. He was doing it daily. He was done with all of this. The focus of his complaining was on the bad around him in the sugar mine. The Man was a major contributor to the crap swirling around, but Gary was becoming a major pooper too. The real problem was staring at him in the glass. It was hard to admit that he was a self-saboteur. It was so easy to blame someone or something else. But honestly, he chose to work in the sugar mine of poop he was complaining about. He was done. He couldn't control the poop floating around but what he could do was focus on himself. That is where the change would happen. He could not control the other people or events in the mine. However, he could choose how he worked and acted.

Taking the poison pill: Who in their right mind would take a poison pill? Well, everyone takes a dose on occasion, and some take the pill multiple times daily. They just don't know they are taking it. Gary didn't either until someone pointed out a bad habit he was swallowing down regularly. He decided that this habit had to go, too. It came in many forms but could be whittled down to simply holding a grudge and harboring resentment. Simply put, someone or something did him wrong. He got mad. He glared at the source, the wrong doer for such an offense. Every time he saw the perpetrator of his anger, he scowled with vengeance and hate. He buried the anger so deeply in his heart, his body pulsated with disgust. It gave him a weird energy and feeling of empowerment to store up so much resentment. He stewed in his own poison. Sometimes, he would be quietly proud about the hate and the ability to harness so much negative, vindictive energy toward someone or something. It was quite uplifting. Unfortunately, the subject of his anger generally had no clue of the generated toxicity and hummed on about the day, unaffected and oblivious.

Every time he saw that "someone" walking around, he shot that look privately. That look that says, "I hope you get what you deserve because of what you did to me." This was the "You Jerk!" look. As he gave the best example of that look that had ever been seen in the world, the subject of that look just passed by, smiling, not even knowing that anything was wrong. He took a poison pill hoping the individual would die, but what he was really doing was poisoning himself. Poisoning himself with animosity and bitterness. What a waste of energy and time when he really thought about it. The fact was that he had to move on. Cut the cord. Label whatever had happened as neither good nor bad but just what it was – something to learn from. He had to forgive. Gary carried this pill around for the Man. The Man was simply and happily clueless to Gary's coy glare. That made Gary swallow yet another pill. If the Man had known that he was having this type of effect on Gary, he would have been quietly satisfied about it. He was just hurting himself. No more poison pills and harboring resentment. He was going to change his perspective and replace the poison pill with a learning opportunity. Gary was a poison pill junkie and by his own estimation, if he replaced the pills with learning opportunities, he would soon be the smartest person on the planet. He decided that every time the poison pill was presented, he would thank, in his mind and in his heart, that someone or something for the lesson and release any resentment. He took an image from the movie Animal House when Chip Diller (Kevin Bacon's character) was being initiated into the fraternity with a paddle whipping, and every time he was smacked with the paddle he would say, "Thank you, sir! May I have another?" That was a bit masochistic, and Gary was too gentle to handle such a paddling, but what he would say when the poison pill was in his hand ready to be swallowed was, "Thank you for the lesson. May I have another?" It took away the power of the poison pill. That was going to be his remedy to moving forward from this habit.

Impatience: This stokes the flames of temper and when combined can leave business relationships in ashes. Impatience was a trait that friends and family could all agree was one of Gary's weaknesses. It led to his quick trigger and short temper. Both characteristics he hated to admit to possessing but admit to he must. Oddly enough he knew the source of this bad and embarrassing habit – the dome that sat between his ears and atop his shoulders. Through his work over the decades at the sugar mine he began to understand an interesting dynamic between his head (mind) and his heart (gut). When he was engaged with a serious problem or issue from his people or his customers, for whatever reason, Gary remained calm, spoke from his heart and turned into a Jedi Knight, gifted with heightened awareness, patience and the ability to harness the force and save the universe from the Dark Side. The Force was the heart. When the heat was on, Jedi Gary was called upon to exercise the patience, care, consideration, vision and awareness to wield a resolution with a surgical strike of the saber (solution). He was good at it and loved that he could harness all those powers, be the best version of himself, see things before they happened and be the hero. What he learned was that he always spoke from the heart when the shit hit the fan. That was why he was successful in handling the heat. Without fail, he would not panic and jump to any mind-induced sabotage. He shut off the impulse of impatience of his mind and acted from his heart. When his impatience and temper flared hot, he noticed that the heat came from his head. He was impulsively overthinking the situation and not instinctually approaching the issue from his heart. He hoped that heightened awareness and deep breathing would resolve his quick and often hot-tempered impulse reactions that came from his head.

Gary was addicted to a fast-paced work environment. His impatience with anything that hindered forward movement was never well-received. Everyone knew Gary operated quickly. He was the hustler. He responded like lightening. He conducted business at the speed of a high-performance German-engineered sports car. He just did. This pace only fostered impatience. He was never very patient with anyone, especially with himself. Because he operated so swiftly, he was often frustrated waiting. He had to wait for answers. He had to wait for a decision. He had to wait on someone or something. Through all the waiting, his head would take over and then he would generally do something spontaneous and dumb. His actions would be seen as impatient and impetuous. Not very good characteristics. Because of the nature of these two wonderful descriptive words, he would often be seen as stirring it up and creating drama. It was never his intent to add drama to anything, but when he was always annoyed and it was bottled up because he was waiting for everyone or everything, he blew and whistled like a tea kettle. If the focus was to be on him and not the noise around him, it was he who had to change this habit. He had to let the process and time unfold naturally. Everything happens on time. He was told once that his impatience was akin to him standing in front of a garden of budding roses and screaming at each bud to, "Open up!" It was great imagery but totally ludicrous.

He had a double dose of the impatient habit problem laying right in front of him. So, he would quit screaming at rose buds and would choose to let situations and the process unfold and naturally when it was time. He was going to be über-mindful of this imagery, take another breath, operate 100 percent of the time from his heart and be Jedi mindful of impatience's Dark Side. Seemed easy enough, right? Gary had no idea how tough this would be!

Whatever the "bad" was, he would just embrace it. If the bad was a habit, a situation, a memory, a worry, whatever it was, he would give it a big hug, be thankful for it, learn from it and get better because of it. He was learning that embracing the bad, as painful and scary as it was, was not as bad as he imagined it would be.

By this time, Gary was exhausted. Taking a deep look within himself was not necessarily fun and it was totally exasperating. God knows why we don't do it very often. Gary was now in a state of super discomfort. This was exactly where he wanted to be. He was losing the binds, the obligations around his comfort, evolving and starting to move forward at the very least.

There was one more item on his change list that he had to address. It was the hardest one, but he knew in his heart that he had a surefire trick up his sleeve to make it happen. He was going to start to forgive. It was one of the hardest things for him to do. Between the impatience, and the poison pill, it was a key to changing it all. If he was going to cut the cord from complaining, resentment, hurt, and anger and quit taking poison pills, he had to do it. Everything he was working to move on from was all tightly rooted together underground; without tending to the rotting roots through forgiveness, the tree would never grow. He couldn't move on if he didn't forgive. He had to let go. The imagery made sense to Gary. How could he move anywhere when he held on to something so tightly? But how to do it? It wasn't until he stumbled upon the "how", that he could finally tackle this big "what": forgiveness. The answer had been right in front of him all the time, blocking his view of the happiness planted firmly on the horizon. That answer was two words: "Thank you."

The words "thank you" would replace his resentment, hurt, anger, complaining and the habit of stewing over the past. As big as this was to overcome, he was not going to make it a big deal. He would decide to spend just a few moments, but those moments would be a daily habit. He would randomly write down three "thank yous" and really focus those sentences of gratitude on what was troubling him the most. But while he did that, he didn't want to forget those wonderful people in his life that deserved appreciation and he wanted to recognize the "little" things that were so often taken for granted. He would say or send at least three "thank yous" a day to whomever was on his mind and heart at that moment. He wrote down the following examples:

He would send a thank you to his wife: "Darling, thank you for the wonderful dinner you cooked for us last night." What she did to provide a wonderful meal every evening was always appreciated, but did she ever feel the depth of that appreciation? Probably not. Well, it was time to express it and get that thanks out there.

He would send a thank you to his son: "Kid, thanks for helping me mow the lawn last Sunday." His son's random act of kindness could not go without acknowledgement.

He would thank one of his people at work: "Thanks, Sara, for taking that call for me yesterday. It is greatly appreciated."

He would thank his mom: "Mom, thanks for being awesome and always there for me." She would later respond with, "Gary, is there something wrong?" in an immediate panicked phone call. "Nothing wrong, mom. Just want to let you know how much I appreciate you in my life," he replied. "Well, don't scare me like that anymore," she laughed back.

He would even thank the Man: "Thank you for the constant questioning. It makes me better and sharpens my approach and skills."

He might send these via text or verbally tell someone or just simply write them down and store them. But they would be expressed and every time he did it, he felt like a million bucks. The people who would get these random thanks would feel the same because what he often got back from them in return was a reciprocal, THANKS!

Thanking would replace the inability to forgive. It was helping him cut the cords from the bad feelings and emotions that were tying him down and it was outwardly showing all the people he loved that he loved them. It made him smile. It made him feel light, even if it was just for a moment. He now had a tool to embrace both the good and the bad in his life. Embrace the bad? What the hell was that all about? But he was ready for it.

The Pearl: Want to change a habit? Going cold turkey can be challenging. Try replacing it with something else and every time you do it, top it off with a small reward. You will begin to think more and more about the reward and that will help you change the habit.

22

THE PEARL THAT DROPS OUT OF THE POOP

Embrace the Bad!

When Gary thought about the incredible lessons in his life, he was beginning to understand what so many others had known long ago. He learned more from his losses than he did from his victories and often, his victories were directly related and a result of his past losses. Losses, bad at the time, were basically good all the time if he was open to the lesson. If he wasn't, then the losses sucked really bad and he never, ever wanted to be associated with them again. Maybe that is why people try to win so badly, at all costs. They either hate the lessons so much that they avoid them, or they do not see the lessons buried in the rubble of the loss.

There was big benefit in the loss, and in the bad, if he was willing to see it. It was obviously excruciating to see the good in the bad while it was happening to him. He either just wanted to fight it or run from it. It was completely natural. Bad made you find courage, real courage. It was the type of bravery that leaves you short of breath and your nerves frazzled. If you could accept the bad at the very moment it was happening, it didn't hurt so much. You could begin to replace the "Why me?" with "This is happening for a reason and one that I will value at some time in my life. I will be able to use this shitty circumstance to my benefit one day."

Gary hated to lose. His hatred made him wonder about his own aversion to it. Was it because he didn't like the lesson or just didn't see the value in the loss? He was a fierce competitor. He was even a poor sport. He was aware of this bad habit and was beginning to change his own perspective on bad. He was so averse to losing that he just got better at what he was doing. Before he began to realize the importance of embracing the bad, he just felt like sheer determination and effort kept the bad and the losses away. What he didn't know was that he was subconsciously taking the lessons from bad and through absolute force of will making sure they never happened again. Those losing lessons were making him better, sharper, more focused and more prepared. He just didn't know it. The weaknesses that he had that helped him lose were being worked on and transformed to strengths. Little did he know the lesson the bad was teaching him. As more bad situations and losses accumulated under his fingertips, he began to understand the wonders and the benefits of loss. Like great works of art that shaped an artist's portfolio and legacy, Gary's grand works of bad were shaping his personal genius.

Sometimes, bad was really bad. It was insufferable, painful, frightening and heartbreaking. Just writing those words doesn't even adequately describe bad. Everyone goes through some sort of variation of unbearable and Gary had his wonderful, fair, heaping helping of it. At the time, he wanted release from it or diversion at his disposal. The diversion generally made the bad he was going through even worse. Furthermore, if he focused on the bad and constantly said, "I have bad luck. My job sucks. My girlfriend dumped me. I am ugly. I have no skills. No one likes me," he attracted worse. It swirled around and through his life like a bumblebee zooming around the honeycomb in a honey-focused oblivion.

So, he experienced it, felt it, attracted it and he was better for it. Yeah! Well, when Gary thought about it, and wrestled with it, as bad as the bad had been in his life, he could point to the tremendous good that came about from all of it. It was very hard to admit, or to even face it and recognize the good that resulted but as he began to accept it, it became more and more true. Could he find the courage to be vulnerable to confront the humbling truth of his bad?

The positive lessons of bad only taught him that if he were open to changing and open to the lesson, things would become easier. Gary was always willing to learn even if he was completely averse to losing or being put in an uncomfortable spot. There were obviously millions of people who have had dozens if not hundreds of bad experiences and never benefitted from those lessons. If he was open to the gifts of the bad, the pearls that dropped out of the poop, his life got better. This didn't mean that Gary wanted to bring on the bad every chance he got because his life would get better. He just knew that things happened – good and bad. His path would take him wherever it would. He would accept the good, the bad and the whatever. He just wanted to recognize it for what it was, learn from it, and get better. Gary eventually got to the point that when something bad happened, he thought to himself, "This is fucking miserable, but what good is going to come out of it? Guess I'll have to wait for it. Hope it's soon because this was terrible." He knew he couldn't force the flower to bloom, but he knew something good would come in its own time.

Bad could be as simple as a burnt toast in the oven, a hangover, or a speeding ticket. The lessons were obvious here, but these types of bad events carried consequences that he had to learn quickly or suffer them again. What Gary was exploring were those times when what came out of the bad was sadness, struggle, anger, loss, or hardship. That bad that was so transformative but also terrifying. Big life changes occurred because of bad.

Gary had several girlfriends in his life and a couple very bad breakups that took years to get over. However, these situations taught him what he really did want and what he didn't want out of love. Every relationship he had afterward benefited from the previous bad breakup because he was not going to put himself through it all again. It was too painful. He was too sentimental and couldn't cut the cords. Remember, he never quit anything and unless the relationship was bad beyond repair, he would probably have stayed in it. He was going to look in the mirror and see what toxicity he contributed to the relationship and change. He was going to look at the person he had just had a relationship with and understand keenly what he wanted and didn't want in a new love.

Gary's dad died of cancer. His dad was his greatest mentor and biggest fan. He loved his dad very much. His dad quietly loved him back. He died too soon, within three months of discovering he had cancer. It was the worst thing Gary had ever been through; he watched as the cancer ravished his dad's body, mind, and soul quickly. Gary had a front-row seat to it all. It crushed his mother as her anchor was taken from her life. It was so sudden, merciless, and heartbreaking. His dad was careless. He didn't go to the doctor, ever. He was either too afraid of what he might find out or thought he was too invincible. He could not conceive that the Grimm Reaper would ever knock on his door, let alone barge in and take his last breath with a snap of his fingers. Gary, after all these years, was still mourning his dad. But because of what happened to his greatest teacher, Gary was super diligent with his own health. He ate right, didn't smoke (like his father), exercised regularly, and visited the doctor every year. Gary was not guaranteed to suffer the same fate as his father or live any more years, but the process of trying and being better was the benefit that fell out of his father's passing. He was also becoming an active and positive role model for his kids to stay healthy and be proactive with their health.

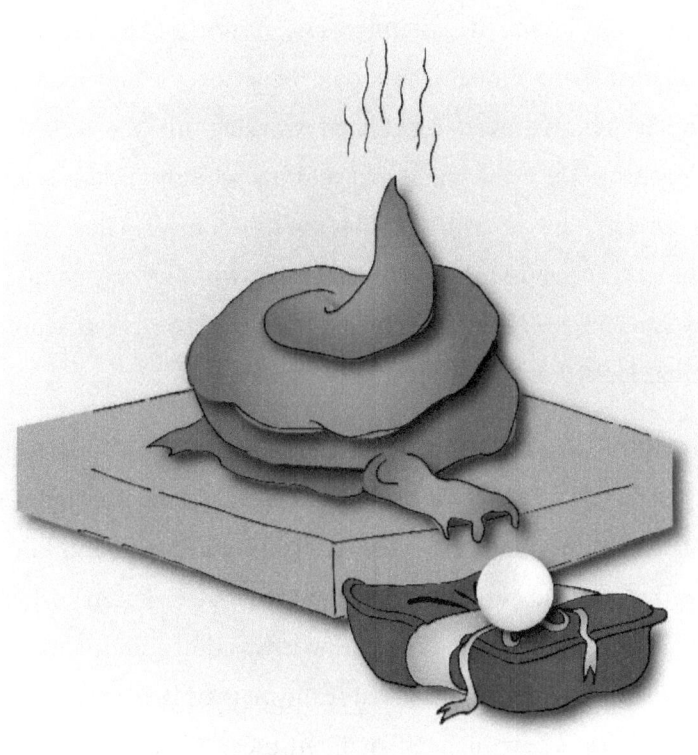

Early in Gary's career, the sugar mine had a contract that contributed to about 80 percent of the company's revenues. It was everything to the organization and to Gary's wallet. He and his team worked the contract diligently and had received great kudos from the clients. Their past performance was exemplary. They were killing it. The contract ultimately came up for bids with fierce competition, and they lost it. They lost it to a good-for-nothing, yellow-bellied, mouth breathing, jerk-wad competitor. It was devastating. The future looked bleak, so bleak that Gary thought he would have to quit and look for another job. He even considered working for the jerk-wad competitor. He went home and told his wife the business and his career were in trouble. They were doomed! They would have to cut spending and really buckle down if he was going to stay and survive. The company cut 50 percent of its workforce. Things looked as bad as Gary had ever seen.

The loss of the contract made the entire operation uncomfortable. While Gary didn't know it then, he later learned that uncomfortable is a badass opportunity to adjust and kill it even more. That was what the company did. It began to look carefully at what it was doing, how it was doing and who was doing all the doing. They looked at the marketplace with a more focused eye. They changed their attitude. The simple act of changing attitude can take everything depressing and make it interesting and filled with opportunity. Suddenly, there were hundreds of opportunities to pursue and hundreds of initiatives to implement. The comfort rust was knocked off by the contract loss and what was underneath was a Ferrari. The Ferrari was turbo charged to grab every opportunity as it tore down a road never traveled by the company before, and it redefined the landscape it was rolling over. The company exploded in growth, people were rehired, more people were hired, and the sugar mine got a fresh coat of paint, new carpet and updated (but not new – the Man wouldn't give them that!) cubicle walls. A juggernaut was formed, and a corporate phoenix rose out of the ashes. This was all a result of three changes: a change in attitude and perspective, being forced into discomfort and embracing the bad.

If Gary was going to accept and embrace the good that came out of the bad, he had to accept the Man too. This one was bitter. Gary had built up an emotional wall around himself to protect himself from the man. He resented the constant scrutiny. He deplored the constant thanklessness and persistent narcissism. Gary's boss was just old-fashioned mean. If one was in the same foxhole as Gary's boss, they were generally in the right one. You didn't want to be in the one staring directly across from him. He was going to eat you alive and have your dog for dessert. Gary was bitter and really contributed to the toxicity of the workplace. He didn't want to admit it. He wanted to be a victim. He was taking two to eight poison pills a day after dealing with the Man. He was learning that it was not the Man who was the enemy; it was himself. The Man was who he was. Gary was never going to change him. He should just accept him for the person he was. He had to be honest with himself. And when he was, he realized something. Oh, he hated to admit it. He wouldn't admit it to anyone until the thought matured more in his head. The Man was one of the greatest teachers in his life. What? Yes! The man he despised for being egotistical, bullying, unrelenting, narcissistic, and uncompromising, was one of his greatest teachers.

The guy that tormented him daily was the reason why Gary had become so good at what he did and earned the living he was. The Man fought Gary on everything. If Gary advised him to turn left, the Man would choose to go right. Sometimes, Gary thought it was just the Man's way to show him who was in control. If the choice was as clear as the water in a crater lake where he could see the bottom from hundreds of feet up, the Man would muddy it up like a bully. There were hundreds of examples of the Man's counter-position to everything. That was Gary's reality. He had to grow the business despite the Man's childlike disobedience and old school ways. He had to protect the Man from himself to give him what he wanted. All this entailed Gary employing a tremendous amount of wit, craftiness, and ingenuity, and approaching an opportunity from every possible angle. Gary had to have all bases covered. The Man's indignity gave him that pearl. It could never be simple and straightforward. Each initiative, action, or whatever he wanted to call it, had to be questioned and double checked. He had to double the thought, the effort, and the analysis. He had to double down on everything. By doing so, he uncovered different ways of doing things – more innovative ways of performing and achieving. He began to look at things from a worst-case scenario first and recognize the Black Swan present in each endeavor. A black swan is a highly improbable event with three principal characteristics: it is unpredictable; it carries a massive impact; and, after the fact, we concoct an explanation that makes it appear less. He was going to prove the Man wrong, and to do that he had to cover all angles to be sure there were zero holes in any action and decision. He had become so scrutinized by the Man that the constant cavity search made his skills sharp. Gary's boss was not doing this to him to compel him to double every effort and provide a strategy with no holes. Gary's boss was doing it just because that was his nature. That was just the type of person the Man was. He had to put his stamp on everything.

Gary had to survive it all day, every day. He couldn't quit. He never quit and to quit over scrutiny would be a big bruise to his own ego. That wasn't a reason to quit. He didn't quit over torture. He was becoming that Jedi he so admired and didn't even know it. They were all reaping the rewards from the Man's unintentional bullying. When Gary stepped out of his bitterness, cut the cord from it, stopped feeling sorry for himself, stopped complaining about how bad the situation was, stopped taking any poison pills, and accepted the fishbowl he chose to do backstrokes in, it all became clear. He was the recipient of a doctorate degree in business from the least likely person in his life – the Man. He was thankful and decided to forgive his professor.

The Pearl: By being humble enough and open to learning, you will see a pearl in every poopy situation, and you will see them as they are happening. Bringing that perspective will lessen the stress of going through the bad situation. Don't wait for time to pass to realize the good that came out of a bad situation. Observe it and be aware of it as it is happening.

23

RIDE SHARE

Gary didn't know what to do. He was trapped in a rut. He couldn't think or dream. He was lost. He was totally in his head. When he thought about his situation, he didn't know whether to run or to hide and when it came right down to it, he didn't do either. He was emotionally stuck. He was intellectually wedged between uninspired and exhausted. He felt like he had tried everything. He was comfortably miserable in this cycle. He wore it like a comfy sweater, all cuddly and cozy. He unintentionally became content in the familiarity of this kind of unhappiness. He wore it like it was normal. But normal sucked!

So, what could he do? He wasn't happy about the situation but didn't know how to change it. He didn't have the foggiest clue. He asked for advice and while his friends and family did their best to give him advice, they offered nothing that resonated. He was frustrating them too. Every time they asked him how he was, they knew the answer before he even replied. He also didn't want to reply because he knew they already knew the answer. They quickly changed to talking about the weather or anything else to get off the topic that would just take them all down the same rabbit hole they had been down over and over again. They wanted him to quit. They couldn't understand why he wouldn't. The job got tired. The Man was an asshole. He wasn't productive. He wasn't happy. It seemed like a really easy decision to make. They were tired of telling him to leave the place. Every conversation they had with him ended with the same question and the same answer – "Gary, why aren't you quitting?", to which Gary would answer, "I don't know."

His crew began to avoid him. He was a drag to be around, and he knew it. He threw on a smile, but the smile was just muscles pulling the corners of his mouth to each ear. There was no joy coming from that smile and he really couldn't get out of his head enough to talk about anything else but the poison pill addiction he was lovingly supporting. Something had to change.

He could wait for the change to be forcefully thrown at him, and there was a part of him that was waiting for that to happen, but when was it going to happen? Seemed like never. He didn't know what to do in the meantime.

There was only one thing he could think of to do. He didn't have much hope or optimism in it, but it was his last "Hail Mary!" to do something, anything to give him a clue. If he was expecting change, well, it wasn't going to happen if he just did the same thing over and over. It wouldn't take much effort and it seemed easy enough. It just required a little initiative. He might as well try something because the same thing wasn't working.

He decided to change his environment. He kept on expecting new results doing and thinking the same thing. What if he fucked with all that a little bit? What if he changed the routine and put it on its head? What if he put himself in a completely different environment? Maybe, just maybe, he might get a new perspective, meet different people, hear, and see different things and come at his problem with a different approach. He could get some inspiration from a stranger and a strange place. It didn't sound like much, and he did not hold out a lot of hope that it would work, but what the fuck did he have to lose? Nothing! As opposed to moving to another city or another country, this move he was going to make had to be just enough to knock off the rust accumulating on his psyche but not be so radical to uproot his entire circle of friends and family. It didn't have to be that disruptive. To change the environment, meet new people and gain that new perspective, he was going to do the one thing that he had ironically experienced during those hundreds of business trips. He was going to trade the back seat ride for the front seat drive. He was going to drive for Uber and Lyft.

It was the easiest thing he could think of to abruptly change his environment and routine without much notice to his current world. He would expose himself to a new world and people he would never encounter in his current world, and it would not be too intrusive to his family or his current daily grind. Neither would really notice, would they?

The Pearl: Want change and don't know how? Step outside of your comfort zone. Do something **out** of routine. It is sure to raise your anxiety but if have the courage to try, you won't regret the experience.

24

INSPIRATIONAL RIDES

Gary had been an Uber or Lyft ride share passenger for years all over the country. He rode in every type of car imaginable driven by every type of person imaginable. Each driver he talked to was driving for a variety of different reasons. A former CEO had lost his job and was just looking to keep his mind off his current unemployment predicament. A single mom was putting in early morning hours before her kids woke up to make some extra money on the side. A young kid was driving 14 hours a day because the money was just better than anything else he could find out there. The stories went on and on, but one thing was certain – while each of these people's situation was interesting to Gary, they were all happily connecting to people, keeping their own schedules, and doing their own thing from the comfort of their own car. Gary had not met one ride share driver who was not pleasant to talk to. He thoroughly enjoyed each of his rides.

Now what would it be like to switch from the back seat to the front seat? He was going to find out. Gary was going down a road he had never gone down before. It didn't seem like much of a big deal, but it was a new road. At the start of all new roads is a bunch of "littles." A little bit of trepidation, a little bit of excitement, and a little bit of discomfort. All welcome "littles" at the starting point. These "littles" were going to help him get through the big issue in his life. He didn't really know it then, but he fucking knows it now!

He filled out the Uber and Lyft applications, uploaded all the documents, grabbed his stickers, and stuck them on the front and back windows of his Mercedes Benz. He was ready to roll. This was going to be fun. This was going to be exactly what he needed to get out of his routine, get out of his head, meet a bunch of people he would never otherwise meet and figure out what the hell he was going to do next. Gary anxiously jumped into his four-door Mercedes Benz SUV. The same car he used mindlessly day-after-day driving to the sugar mine. Now this car was going to take him for a different ride. A ride that would legitimately change his life forever.

He drove out toward the city. It was a sunny Saturday afternoon. The Lyft and Uber apps on his phone were scanning for riders. Gary glanced at the Uber and Lyft stickers on the front windshield. There was nothing like a high-priced German sports car with ride share stickers smacked in the bottom right-hand corner of the window. He had a little tension in his body. He really had no clue how a ride request came or how he even accepted the ride request? So, he drove and drove, checking the apps on his phone about every 5 seconds. Nothing. It had been about 20 minutes and not one request? What the heck was going on? Did he have the apps on correctly? He checked. He did. He drove to a vacant parking lot where, for some reason, the only "parkers" were a group of ducks. Hanging out with ducks in a parking lot on a Saturday afternoon was not exactly what he had in mind. So, he sat there. He fiddled with the radio and watched the ducks. Another 30 minutes went by. His Uber and Lyft career was not getting off to a great start. What was he doing? He could be home hanging out with the family or even rearranging his sock drawer. Wasting away a Saturday! At least, he had the ducks.

The first alert request from Uber finally came in. His phone went off flashing and buzzing. Woohoo, he was in business! A shot of adrenaline went right through him. Because he had both the Lyft and the Uber apps on at the same time, he had to accept the ride with Uber and quickly switch to the Lyft app and turn that one off. He proceeded to turn Lyft off, switch back to Uber and accidentally cancelled the ride.

He accidentally pressed the wrong button in the frenzy and excitement. Nice. had some choice words for himself, slumped back into his seat, rolled his eyes as he settled his stare back on the ducks in the parking lot who were completely oblivious to what he just went through. Why wasn't he a duck? They looked content and happy waddling around the yellow stripes in the parking lot. It didn't take long for the app to fire again. Lyft was flashing and buzzing. This time, he took a deep breath, accepted the ride first, flipped over to the Uber app, turned it off and put his car in drive.

Okay, he would be lying if he said he was fine. He was nervous doing this. C'mon! This was driving, picking up people and taking them to the spot the GPS told you. What the hell was so nerve wracking about that? Well, he had never done it before, for one thing. Nothing was familiar. Nothing was comfortable. But he felt good, really good.

Unfamiliar + Uncomfortable = Feeling Alive!

The voice from the app said, "Pick up Jesus on the right." Gary took a double take at the app. Jesus? Jesus was taking a ride share service? When he pulled up to Jesus standing outside a senior living home, it was a Mexican American man, who just got done pulling a 16-hour shift, going home. Gary's first ride was taking Jesus home from a long day's work at a senior living center.

Jesus was an interesting older guy. He was putting in 16-hour days at two senior living centers to make ends meet, provide for his family, and get his older daughter through college. He pushed all his kids and his grandkids to excel in school, go to college and graduate. He didn't want the life he had lived for his kids. He was a self-touted hell raiser when he was a "kid." He drank and did drugs. He slept around with many women. He dropped out of school. He ran with the wrong crowd. He went to jail. He still seemed to be sentimental about those alpha-male, hell-raising days but knew he never ever wanted to go back to them. There was no way he wanted that life for his kids either. Because of those days, he was going to have to grind out "16s" for the rest of his life.

Gary was impressed with this guy. For over 20 years the man told him he worked like this to make up for the transgressions of his adolescence. His family was not going to go through what he went through. His family was going to have a better life for the decisions he was making now and the work he was putting in. Wow! What dedication! What inspiration! This guy was just doing it. He was making up for his mistakes. Ge was creating a better life for his family. He was a real hustler!

"Jesus, you are amazing man," Gary said.

"What? Why is that bro?" Jesus responded with surprise.

"You're just doing it for your family, man. It is so impressive. I admire what you are doing," Gary said while looking in the rearview mirror seeing Jesus' eyes open wider in confusion.

"Well, thanks man. I appreciate that. No one has ever said that to me before," Jesus said.

Gary got his next ride at a vet clinic in a strip mall. The middle-aged woman that came out of the office looked frantic. Her arms wrapped around a bunch of papers, files, and a large box of dog biscuits. She was the owner. She had a rough day. Back in the day this woman most certainly turned heads. She was beautiful, but it looked like the job and life was putting tire tracks all over her body. She was stuck running the business because the doctor, her ex-husband, decided he didn't want to "vet" anymore. He left the business and left her. She was now hustling to find doctors to fill the promises on the door sign. Another real hustler!

"You know Linda, to pick it up like you have and just make it work with all the things you have gone through in your life is really an amazing thing," Gary told her.

Surprised, Linda responded, "Well, thank you. That is so nice to hear. I am just trying to survive, you know."

"I think you are doing more than just surviving," Gary responded. "I think you are an example for everyone. You should really take pride in that."

As the first day zoomed along, the chaos of the city traffic took a back seat to Gary's conversations with his customers. It was wild. It was really rewarding. They were like a lightbulb flash in his eyes. They left as soon as they came into his life, but they all left a little imprint on him like the flash of a camera bulb does when you look right at it when it goes off.

Angel. Gary won't forget that name or her story. Angel was a twenty-something year-old woman catching a Lyft to her job as a hostess at a local restaurant. Gary asked Angel what she wanted to do for a living.

"I would love to be a coroner," she said.

"Really? Why? You would be dealing with dead people every day, Angel."

"I have always had a connection with dead people. I have never been frightened or scared of them. Ever since I was a little girl, I could see them. When I was a little girl, I played with two friends who I learned were only visible to me. They were completely real to me. I never thought of them as ghosts or anything like that. I played with them every day. There was a boy, Charlie, and a girl, Emily. My playing with them freaked my mom out so badly that she had me taken to a hospital and tested. They never found anything wrong with me. My mom was petrified of what I was doing and seeing, and always told me that I had to stop. Stop what? They were my friends, and they were as real as you driving me in this car. The two 'imaginary' kids were not a figment of my imagination as my mom would always say. They were my best friends."

Angel went on to tell Gary about one frightening afternoon.

"When I was 6, I was in our backyard and decided to swing. The swing faced the back of our house. I jumped onto the seat and began to go back and forth until I felt a firm push behind me. I thought it was my mom but when I looked back behind me, no one was there. When I looked toward the house, I saw that my mom was in the kitchen window washing dishes. Another push sent me swinging forward and startled me. I swung back and then was forcibly pushed forward again. I yelled for my mom but when I saw her in the kitchen window, I saw that Charlie was standing behind her with his hands on her ears holding her head down toward the sink. She couldn't hear me or see me. I yelled again but nothing changed. Charlie was holding my mom's head firmly down with his hands over her ears. So, I jumped off the swing and landed very hard on my right leg. I screamed in pain, but my mom didn't respond. I crawled to the back door and began to bang on it, yelling for my mom. My mom finally came running to the door frantically wondering what had happened.

"Angel, what happened?"

"Mom, I hurt my leg."

"Why didn't you call for me, Angel?"

"Mom, I did. I don't think you could hear or see me because when I called for you, I saw Charlie standing behind you with his hands on your ears holding your head down to the sink."

Gary was completely lost in the story as he pulled up to the drop off point outside the restaurant. Before Angel got out of the car, she told Gary that she heard a rumor that in the 1920s a mother had killed her two children in that same house. She always wanted to go back to that house and see if her friends were still there and if the story was true.

Gary pulled around the restaurant, parked his car and turned off his Uber and Lyft apps. He just sat there looking out the windshield. He would have never been exposed to such a person or such a story without completely choosing to do something he never would have done before. He was inadvertently getting quick slivers of people's lives in these rides. They would jump in his car and flat out share a piece of their lives with a perfect stranger. And Gary was doing the same thing. These connections were really uplifting, and they got him out of his own head and centered into his heart. He felt a feeling of quiet satisfaction.

Gary decided to call it a day and drive home. Angel's ghost story made the hair on the back of his arms stand straight up. This was a wild experience and Angel's story did something profound to him. It made him want to jump in the car and do it again the next day.

Gary was testing his hunch to break him out of the mental and emotional doldrums his current situation had put him in. Even though these people's stories had zero to do with Gary's own world, they loosened the grip that was paralyzing him. He was beginning to think about the "possibilities" of his current situation and his future instead of feeling sorry for himself because of all the "challenges" he was faced with.

It was just driving. There were a lot of people around Gary who would tell him that he was putting too much depth and emotional equity into just driving. Gary didn't listen to them.

This was no different from taking a crane operator and putting him in a bakery for a day, taking a CEO and putting her in a soup kitchen or having her pick up trash. This was all about exposure and the incredible benefits that came with it. This was about rocking the routine. This was about shaking it up to get a different perspective so that routines were upended, and perspectives were shifted.

The second day of driving cemented Gary's newly found habit of driving regularly.

Zach jumped into the back of Gary's car on a cold rainy night in downtown. It was a miserable evening. Rain, sleet, and snow had clogged the roads and made just about every driver on the road downright ornery. Gary was trying to keep his wits together jockeying around town and thinking about his job and what he was going to do with the Man, his situation, and his unhappiness. It was a lot to juggle and weighed heavily on his mind. Stress pulsed through his body so much so that his stomach hurt. When he had a rider, his mind jumped off his own problems. He was thankful for the riders' interruptions to his racing mind. Zach would put it all into perspective.

"Hey Zach. How's it going tonight?" Gary started.

"I'm headed for AA," said Zach.

"Okay, no problem," Gary responded, thinking he probably had to change the subject. "You from here?"

"No, I am from Pennsylvania. I came out here for a job opportunity that promised free room and board. I thought that was perfect. I was looking for a new start and needed a job and a place to stay. The job ad said that all you had to do was put in 20 hours and they would promise a place to sleep."

What Zach didn't know was that the job was selling meds out of a van and the floor of that van was where you slept. As a former addict, Zach had to quit that job, or he was going to find himself right back in the place he started. He was very depressed that he was duped into a scam and was so far away from home.

"I am really screwed. I shouldn't have put all my eggs in this basket. I knew it was too good to be true. I am an idiot! I don't know what I am going to do. I have no money. I have no place to stay. I am so far from home. My mom back home was the one that ordered the ride for me. I just don't know what to do."

"Man, I am so sorry to hear about this. That sucks!" Gary said. "But the fact that you are going to AA and not going back down the road that could be so much easier for you, says a lot about you, man. I don't know you that well, but I am proud of what you are doing tonight. It shows a lot of guts and a lot of character. I promise that there is a pearl in this shitty situation somewhere. There is a reason why you were here now and based on what you are doing tonight, staying away from that familiar path, you will make it, man."

"Thanks, man! I appreciate that. I am trying to be strong," Zach said, with a shaking voice.

When they pulled up to AA, Gary reached into his wallet and took all the money he had and gave it to Zach. He told him he would be thinking about him. Stunned, Zach's 'thank you' came out quivering. Zach had tears in his eyes. Gary felt, for some reason, he was meant to pick Zach up that night. He hoped he had made a difference.

The next morning Gary headed out to hit the morning rush hour. He woke up to a blizzard. His first ride was for a single mom from New York who was being judged by her friends for being single. She felt so betrayed. What was she going to do? The dad left her for a younger woman. Gary then picked up Ted who was just out of the Army and making computer repair house calls to earn a living. Ted was busy going all over town. Uber was his means of commuting. Gary also picked up a young woman heading to Pittsburg for a job interview. She found the right driver. Gary had been conducting interviews for over 20 years. She got lots of tips on how to interview. The woman gave him a $7 tip and said she felt like she was well prepared to go get herself a job.

Light was beginning to spread across the grey morning. The sun was coming up, but it was nowhere to be seen. The morning drive had been tricky, dodging all the cars stuck on the side of the road, and the pace of the traffic rolling over all the snow and ice was slow.

It took Gary about half an hour to get to his next request. He passed two accidents and a school bus that had slid off the road. Eric was a 35-year-old who seemed more like he was 19, especially by the way his life was unfolding. He was literally making mistakes repeatedly, not learning from them and then doing it all over again. Maybe it was because of his looks – he was a good-looking guy. He had the type of square jaw and perfect nose that would turn any girl's head. Gary was driving him to his first day of work at a custom motorcycle paint shop. Two previous Uber drivers had cancelled on him, and his roommate bagged out because of the poor driving conditions. So, it was up to Gary. Eric jumped into the car in a worried frenzy. Gary could feel his nervous energy.

"I am so screwed," Eric said as he slid into the back seat. "I am going to be so late, man. I should already be there. I would have just called in because I couldn't get a lift with this blizzard, but I need to do whatever I can to go to my first day. I can't make a bad impression."

This guy needed the job. He had just moved to town for a new start from a dramatic girlfriend situation in another state. Gary and Eric really hit it off. They had a strange and cool connection. They talked about self-sabotage, women, drinking and doing the same thing over and over. They had this chance because the snow was falling in sheets from the sky, the roads were icy and what would have taken 20 minutes on a normal day was turning into an hour and a half.

Eric had just left a girl in Minnesota. A girl who resembled all the other kinds of girls he had dated throughout his life – bad girls. They gave him energy in a way that didn't serve him, but he was so attracted to it. He was familiar with it. Ah, familiarity...the devil in disguise! He couldn't stop seeing that type of girl. They wanted to change him. They brought the daily drama, and he took a swim in it. They cheated on him. He knew about it but went along with it anyway. He consciously ignored his instincts and just went along for the ride with these bad girls. It was the ride that he connected to 'living', the drama. Without it, life was just boring. He just continually repeated these relationships because they fed him that energy. That energy that a lot of people just live on and die from. It made him feel alive. He topped the energy off with a nightly bottle of whiskey which just compounded all his problems and resuscitated the energy he so desperately wanted to get away from. He wasn't living a vicious cycle; he was the vicious cycle, and he didn't know how to quit. This sounded all too familiar. Eric said that he had found a new girl in town here. She was everything the others weren't. She didn't try to change him. She didn't cheat on him. She took care of him. But she didn't give him that jolt that the others had either. All she did was support him. He was getting bored with the relationship, and it freaked him out. She loved him and uplifted him. Was he thinking that she was just easy and kissing his ass? She probably wasn't, but Gary thought that was the way Eric took it. He needed to rewire himself if he was ever going to stop the cycle. He needed to cut the cord and jump away from those habits that made him feel alive but didn't serve him. It hit Gary right between the eyes that he was driving a guy much like himself. Addicted to energy, especially negative, in-your-face energy. Addicted to drama. Addicted to self-sabotage.

As Gary began to pull up to the garage warehouse where Eric's new career was going to start, Eric asked Gary to drop around the corner, out of site of the front door.

"I need a smoke. I am so late. Ugh. I need to calm down," Eric said.

"Listen, we just drove 20-miles through an absolute blizzard. There is nothing you should be concerned about. What you did to get here and not just blow it all off says a lot about you Eric. I am sorry, but I have managed a lot of people in my life who have not shown the dedication that you showed getting here today." Before Eric left the car after that hour and a half 20-mile ride through a blizzard, Gary asked him a question.

"Eric, you are a little over an hour late for your first day at this place. What could be good about that?"

"Well, I met a fucking cool Uber driver! That's for sure," Eric said.

Gary smiled and thanked him. "But Eric, we have talked about a lot of stuff – two strangers in a snowstorm. Let me tell you this. There is always a pearl that drops out of the poop. Everything in your life that you reflect on that was a bad time or a challenging time, you can point to something valuable that came out of it. Take today for example. It started out stressful. But we met, connected and had an awesome conversation even though you are still late for work. Here is all you have to tell your boss. Change the narrative of the "first-day-late-to-work" situation you are in and shift it to your advantage. Tell your boss that it was super challenging to get in today, but nothing was going to stop you from getting in. First, it's the truth. Second, that is how you take the pearl in the poop and use it to your advantage. You will impress your boss today, no doubt."

"Thanks man. I appreciate the perspective. I'll give it a shot," Eric said.

"You got this man," Gary responded. "Go kick ass!"

While Gary gave input to his riders, his riders gave him advice about his own situation. Gary shared the whole story when he could. That advice was not so much different from the words his friends and family had been telling him for the past 10 years.

The Pearl: Whatever it is, do something completely different. Change your environment and routine, even if it just a small change. You cannot expect your situation to change unless you make a change to the setting you have been living, breathing, and working in.

25

TAKING THE LEAP

Quitting without another job or opportunity waiting is like jumping out of the plane without a parachute. Gary never felt more appreciated by the Man than the day he told the Man "Goodbye." The Man was pissed. "I'll bury you. You won't work anywhere else in this industry ever again. I'll make sure that never happens," said the Man with the intensity of a tiger stalking a goat. Gary was the goat. The Man would never admit it, but his anger wasn't driven by resentment. It was driven by complete fear. In the old Man's own mind, he made Gary and gave him everything. He would be nothing without him. He had taught him everything. He was completely responsible for all the success Gary had. Quitting was a betrayal, a slap in the face of an ingrate. Gary knew the old Man had taught him a lot. But most of those lessons were unintentional gifts. The late Friday talks taught Gary to be knowledgeable about every angle. The constant scrutiny drove Gary to succeed in the face of all the skepticism. He was not going to let the old Man beat him or tell him, "I told you so." All the times the Man made him go solo into a raging customer disaster, not because he had this incredible belief in Gary, but he just didn't want to spend the dollars sending a team to address the issue, gave Gary the confidence that he could face anyone or any issue alone. He became a master of diplomacy while the Man continued to demonstrate his intimidation and anger to Gary's salespeople and partners. Gary had to learn quickly how to smooth things over while not compromising the Man's sinister demeanor. All the tasteless jokes, sexist comments, and bigotry that came from the Man had to be managed by Gary. He got really good at it. "The Man did make me better. Wow! I must thank him."

Gary did thank him the day he quit. While the Man took it one way, Gary knew that the narcissist would never truly understand all the ways he had helped him. Regardless, none of it mattered on Gary's last day.

The last gesture, the final parting gift the Man would give Gary happened right before he left his office.

"Hey, wait one second, Gary."

Gary thought that the Man was going to thank him for his contribution and wish him good luck in his future endeavors.

"Here, take this," the old Man said.

Gary looked down and reached for a book the Man handed to him.

"It's my autobiography. I just finished it," the Narcissist said.

Another lesson. How to smile, say thank you and walk away with grace.

The book never made it outside the sugar mine. Gary found a comfortable spot for it at the bottom of the trash can going out the building door. This was about cutting all ties with the monster that had haunted him and only having gratitude for the experience, looking forward and smiling.

The Pearl: Quit and Win! Quitters are NOT losers!

FREE AT LAST

The first step was to look at his next 30 days. He took out a pad of paper and wrote, "What challenges do I have over the next 30 days?" He furiously jotted down everything that came to mind. He had no idea how to accomplish most of the items that made up the daunting list. He knew they had to be done. He managed the process. Now he had to do the process. Anxiety swept over him. How? He started to think about the end point. Maybe if he started at the destination and worked his way back to where he was now, the path forward could become clearer. What do I want to do? What do I want to be? I am just going to dream big! What other choice did he have? So, he looked out into his future, peeled away all the limitations and objections and let his imagination run wild. He wrote down everything that came to mind. Some thoughts caught him by surprise. Sitting on top of a turtle herding empire. Wow! Who knew that was something he quietly aspired to do? Once he felt like he had narrowed down what he wanted to do and what he wanted to be, he sat back and stewed on it a bit. He marinated in the thought, the feeling, and the reality that he was moving forward to happiness. The uncomfortable road to that happiness was going to test everything he knew. But he also embraced the "uncomfortable" situation. When he got through it, he would realize the valuable and immeasurable lessons the uncomfortable journey would prove to be. He was going to go down this road on his own. He was not going to give advice to anyone else who might be in the same situation and would not demonstrate any sort of arrogant swagger on the way to happiness. Everyone has advice. Just ask someone. It was as common as pulling lint out of his pants' pocket. He would be confident and humble.

Every time he got into the car, he stepped out of his comfort zone. Every time someone new hopped into the back seat, he stepped into his discomfort zone. Every time he went down a street he had never been down before, he stepped into his "uncomfortable" zone. And he was happy, so happy.

He picked up a woman going to a training session at a local hotel. He asked her if it was in support of a profession. She just said that it was a training around "negotiating." She hated the thought. She was a non-confrontational person and negotiating just screamed, "confrontation!" The all-day training that started the day before and led to the all-day training today was emotionally exhausting on her. She said one key thing that resonated with Gary about his first day of driving after quitting the sugar mine. "This training is putting me out of my comfort zone." Gary jumped at the chance to tell her how awesome it was that she was doing this and that the more she did it, the better she would get and that this would not be an uncomfortable thing in her life when she got done. He told her to envision that the "uncomfortable" was a big fluffy teddy bear and to go up and hug it. He said that she was going to kill it today and that he admired her courage for pushing her comfort zone.

"Are you seriously just an Uber driver?" she asked.

"Yep, I am an Uber driver. We got skills, don't we?" he said smiling as she got out of his car. "Good luck. Go knock it dead!"

He picked up a 28-year-old kid at the airport coming home for a week from a two-week stint in the oil field in Nowheresville, Nevada. The guy had put in 84 hours in those two weeks. He was going to work there for another two years and then take the skills he gained and use them to build a career. Gary told him that it sounded like a great idea. He told the young man he was a hustler and that anyone who told him otherwise would be dead wrong. Gary told him that he should be proud of himself. Gary's sugar mine seemed pale in comparison. Working through the night, in blizzards, in the baking sun and then bunking with a bunch of co-workers made Gary's mine seem like an amusement park. The people who take these types of jobs don't have a lot going for them. This isn't necessarily a type of job you just took unless there weren't many choices before you. The fact that this guy was sucking it up, sticking to it, and planning to take what he was learning from this incredibly physically demanding job and building a future was incredible. Gary shared a little of what he endured at the Mine with the 28-year-old kid. The "kid" responded to Gary with his own words of encouragement.

"You hang in there, man," the kid said. Gary thought those were awesome words of advice. It really meant a lot.

Those slivers of life they shared with him that darted in and out of his backseat passenger door were a relief. From job seekers and CEOs to bar hoppers and a woman whose best friend got pregnant by her father, Gary was thankful for his newly found gig. These riders who spent just a fraction of their lives in the backseat of his car made him happy. It was a mutual "give and take" relationship. One that he would promote until they wrestled the steering wheel from his dead cold hands.

The sugar mine – one of the best things he ever did in his life was to join the company. It taught him business and what he needed to do to run an operation, engage a challenge, maneuver, and create an opportunity. It taught him how to persevere in the face of narcissism and survive constant scrutiny to become a professional somebody. And one of the best things he ever did was quit. Taking the lessons learned for two decades, he knew what he wanted and probably more importantly, what he didn't want. He decided to leave the bitter aftertaste of the place behind – it was tough. He would be lying if he told anyone otherwise. Maybe that was one of the reasons why quitting was so hard in the first place. He invested so much time and heart into something and it was no longer going to be a part of his life. He was sentimental about it all, even the bad stuff. Cutting the sentimental cord was a big part of quitting. What he learned was that if you want to get on with living, there was no room for sentimentality. Gratitude could replace it and slice the cord cleanly.

The Pearl: Comfort is just as dangerous as fear. One you allow yourself to be embraced by and one you run from. Both equally undermine YOU. **Embrace discomfort and watch growth happen.**

27

THE LANDING

When Gary's feet touched the ground, the exhilaration that left with him as he jumped out of the plane was still invading every inch of his body when he landed. To say he was smiling from ear-to-ear was an understatement. His smile could have been seen from the moon! Gary's descent down to mother earth was a complete exercise in just letting go. It was something he had never done. He didn't have much choice, did he? Letting go. Wasn't that just the key to it all? It was the vital step to happiness. Letting go of expectations, resentment, anger, fear, habits, judgements, anxiety, stress, beliefs, perceptions and a million other nouns that didn't necessarily serve him. Letting go allowed a clear conscience and peace. It was time to change the grip on life and use new tools. Tools that would allow him to work with the challenges and opportunities of life. It was going to take practice, a lot of practice. His thoughts and behaviors were as familiar as a bad golf swing. Trying something new would mean letting go of the familiar and comfortable. He was going to try and do things that felt unfamiliar and uncomfortable, and he was just going to have to trust that these new ways, although completely foreign to his entire system, were going to be right and if they weren't, he would reserve the right to pivot and try something else that was out of his "normal." He would trust that if he went forward with honest and true intent, then whatever he experienced and ended up with was what was meant to be. Giving up control and letting it go felt right. He was done suffering failures before he even tried. While his mind was freaking out about this new move, his gut was never more convincing. He would follow his gut as his dad always told him and let the future open up to the possibilities. Happiness was waiting.

If you are stuck, whatever it is, do something completely different. Change your environment. Change your schedule. You cannot expect anything to change unless you change the world you have been living in. Even when you don't feel like doing a damn thing. Do it!

The Pearl: Be the President of your own fan club. Why not? What else do you have to lose?

CONCLUSION

We only have one life to live, and yet we trade our precious time for a job and a career that we hate. Why? After 25-years as a senior sales executive, I found that it all has to do with a partnership between two words that I could never imagine were joining forces to stop us from reaching our potential, be free, be happy and to kick butt: comfort and fear.

Comfort is the sneaky devil in all of it. Who would have known that it was the one word that we all yearn for but the one word that, while it signifies that we have all that we need in this life (safety, food, shelter, love), stops us from growing, learning, achieving, and being truly happy? We are lulled to sleep by comfort. We compromise everything for it; even when dealing with narcissistic bosses that rob 8-10 hours a day from us. Comfort builds impenetrable walls around our lives in the name of keeping us secure and safe. The word doesn't even let us think about venturing out from those walls unless we muster enough personal courage and make decisions based on trust and faith.

Fear is easy to see and feel. We want nothing to do with it and getting out of our comfort zone is one sure fire way to stare fear in its beady little eyes. One look at fear and we turn and run right back to comfort's fortress. Fear makes us insecure, lose our confidence and builds enough anxiety within us to fuel a power plant and keep us in one place. Fear is so uncomfortable that it is no wonder we love comfort and exchange our happiness and full potential for it. It is just too scary to completely believe in ourselves and then go after our dreams without compromise.

If dealing with the double-edge sword of the fear-comfort blade wasn't enough to keep us in one place, quitting in the face of a challenge and adversity would be surely to do it. It is downright offensive to quit. While society will allow us to quit a bad habit, it will not allow us to quit a difficult situation. If we do, we are seen as weak. We are judged and pressured to fight through what's hard. There may be some validity to this when it comes to achieving a magnificent goal we set for ourselves. But for a job and a boss? Sorry, all of that is irrelevant. We do not have to persevere through a bad job, EVER. If our job is not serving us, meaning we are not happy doing the work we were hired to do, we need to do ourselves and everyone around us a monumental favor and get the hell out of there. We aren't weak if we do. We have the courage to make our happiness the number one priority. We have one life. That's it. Spending it enduring a bad job and a bad boss is unconscionable.

Shed comfort's safety blanket. Kick fear's insecurities in the mouth. Forget the cultural taboo about quitting. Embrace the bad that you are going through, recognize the "pearl" that is sitting there waiting to teach you. Believe in yourself even if it feels like you are fooling yourself and run to happy. It's a simple equation. Do you have the guts to let go and take that leap? I think you do!

LEAVE A 1-CLICK REVIEW!

I would be incredibly thankful if you could take just 60 seconds to write a brief review on Amazon, even if it's a few sentences.

A Special Gift To Our Readers

The SWOT Checklist

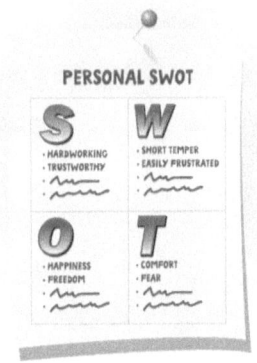

Included with your purchase of this book is our personal SWOT Challenge. This challenge will strategically help you discover what you want the next step in your life to be.

Click the link below and let us know which email address to deliver it to.

www.quitandwin.com

ACKNOWLEDGMENTS

I have had a lot of help writing this book. All the bad situations, encounters, and experiences I have had throughout my career and my personal life deserve much of the credit for this effort. When I first began to realize the value in "bad occurrences" that happened in my life, I found a way through almost every challenge I encountered. It blew my mind! Instead of being a victim when a "bad occurrence" happened, I recognized how to embrace the bad at the time it was happening, accept it, look for the lesson it was teaching me, as painful as it was sometimes, and use it for all the value it possessed. All I needed to do was to recognize them. I would never be the same.

This book would have never been possible without the incredible support of my family. They have had a front row seat for it all and they continue to cheer me on. I am truly grateful for their belief, support and love. My wife has been at center stage for it all and I am so grateful for our friendship and our partnership. Ironically, she was the pearl that came out of a very challenging situation I was in over 25 years ago. She might be the greatest good that came out of any of the bad that has happened in my life.

I have to thank all the friends that I discussed many of the concepts in this book with over a cup of coffee, a bottle of beer, on the golf course and watching our favorite sports teams play ball. Their ideas, thoughts and input have been an immeasurable positive influence on my life. I am very grateful for each and every one of them.

I must thank the effort, care, and attention to detail to two particular people that brought this book to life:

Dr. Amy DeWitt is an incredible woman I met several decades ago in a faraway land whom I have always admired for her style, incredible positivity, sense of humor, uncanny insight and dynamite English writing ability. Her work and the hours she graciously offered in editing this book have been invaluable. I am so appreciative of you, Dr. DeWitt!

Rudy Eccher, the illustrator in this book, is a brother from another mother. His artistic talent has always amazed me. What he can do with a pen and a paint brush in just a matter of seconds has always inspired me. Thank you, Rudy, for accepting the request to illustrate this book. Your insight, interpretation and work just made it all better. It was great working on this project with you.

Joe

ABOUT THE AUTHOR

Joseph Cohen has been a successful sales leader and business strategist for over 25 years, but it didn't come without its bumps. He has been bloodied, battered, and bruised by employee issues, market developments, business operations and narcissistic leaders…and has become better for it. Without all the abuse, there would be nothing to share with you. He is humbled by all the good that comes out of the bad (the pearl out of the poop) and uses those experiences to teach, consult and help people and businesses get better.